Classroom Confidential

Related titles

Managing Very Challenging Behaviour – Louisa Leaman

Teacher's Survival Guide: 2nd Edition – Angela Thody, Derek Bowden and Barbara Gray

Guerilla Guide to Teaching – Sue Cowley

Classroom Confidential

Hints and Tips from an Insider

Louisa Leaman

continuum
LONDON • NEW YORK

Continuum International Publishing Group
The Tower Building   15 East 26th Street
11 York Road   New York, NY 10010
London
SE1 7NX

www.continuumbooks.com

British Library Cataloguing-in-Publication Data
A catalogue record for this book is available from the British Library.

ISBN: 0–8264–8541–3 (paperback)

Library of Congress Cataloging-in-Publication Data
A catalog record for this book is available from the Library of Congress.

Typeset by YHT Ltd, London
Printed and bound in Great Britain by MPG Books Ltd,
Bodmin, Cornwall

Contents

Introduction   viii

Part 1: Teacher Approach

1   What works?   3
    Be firm   4
    Be fair   7
    Be calm   10
    Be consistent   12
    Be positive   13
2   Styles to avoid...   15
    The dragon   15
    The mouse   17
    The pupil's 'friend'   18
    The foe   19
    The uncommitted   20
3   Talents you never knew you had...   23
    Entertaining   23
    Conflict resolving   24
    Delegating   25
    Inspiring   26
    Empathizing   26

Part 2: Lesson Structure and Content

4   Keeping them motivated...   31
    Providing a challenge   31
    Making it interesting   33
    Differentiation   35
    Setting targets   38
    Pacing tasks   39
    Being flexible   41

5 Keeping yourself motivated ... 43
Planning and preparation 43
Organizing your workload 45
Pacing your workload 47

Part 3: Routines and Procedures

6 Five essentials ... 53
Beginnings 54
Endings 55
Moving about the classroom 57
Getting attention 58
Solving conflict 61
7 Establishing boundaries ... 63
Class rules, rights and responsibilities 63
Repetition 65
Reward systems 68
Sanctions 74
The sliding scale of intervention 75

Part 4: The Classroom Environment

8 Organized chaos or chaotic organization ... 81
The tidy room 81
The inspirational room 83
The functional room 84
Physical comfort 85
'Hot'–classing 87

Part 5: Managing Behaviour

9 Helpful techniques ... 91
Eyes in the back of your head (being aware) 92
Growing an extra pair of hands (using
support/teaching assistants) 94
Becoming a mind-reader (understanding difficulties) 96
10 Crowd control ... 99
The 'off' class 99
Dominant groups 108
Bullying in gangs 109

Mixed-ability classes	112
Taming a mob	115
11 Dealing with individuals . . .	119
Withdrawn students	121
Attention seekers	123
Students that are 'full-of-beans'	126
The bad socialite	129
Reluctant workers	132
'Cling-ons'	135
Ringleaders	138
The easily led	141
Conclusion	145

Introduction

The information in this book is inspired by actual teaching. Having worked in both special and mainstream schools as a teacher of students with emotional, social and behavioural difficulties, I became an advisory behaviour support teacher in east London. This entailed carrying out classroom observations of teachers who were seeking advice on managing a difficult student or group of students, and then providing strategy ideas and support in implementing them.

I have, therefore, spent time as a 'fly-on-the-wall' in many different classrooms, catering for a variety of subjects and age groups – from young children to school leavers, from numeracy to drama. More often than not, the teachers I observe are skilled and able professionals; it is sometimes a case of reinforcing what they already know, giving them back their confidence. For other teachers, it is a matter of looking at a problem from another angle, trying a different approach or breaking an unhelpful cycle of behaviour.

A lot of my work is with Newly Qualified Teachers, who find themselves plunged into the deep end of classroom practice. They are often motivated and keen to take on challenges; and while they lack the experience, and all too often, the training, to tackle challenging behaviour with confidence, they welcome the additional advice and support I can give them.

It is a role that has given me a fascinating insight into teacher style and approach and, above all, has enabled me to clarify some of the key things that make for effective classroom practice. Although I focus on behaviour management, I am aware that success in this area is dependent on a variety of factors within the classroom. Therefore, in this book you will find advice on establishing routines, planning effectively and organizing the classroom space, as well as tackling difficult behaviour. I aim to provide guidance that is practical, no-nonsense and workable. It is based on the valuable principles of emotional intelligence and respect for all.

While advisory behaviour support work is happily on the increase, there is still a limit as to how many classrooms and teachers can access the resource. I hope that this book will contribute to overcoming this limitation, and prove useful to those who are seeking some guidance on getting to grips with the rigours of the modern classroom. It may also make you laugh – a sense of humour, after all, is perhaps the most useful asset a teacher can have!

Part 1

Teacher Approach

1 What works?

One of the most important ingredients of successful classroom management is an effective student–teacher relationship. Watching how teachers with very different styles and personalities relate to their flock has shown me just how important it is: whether they are trying to assert themselves on a whole class, trying to motivate a particular student or trying to generate some interest in a new topic. If respectful and trusting relationships are not in place, it can be difficult for the teacher to get what they want. How they communicate, how they express themselves, how they respond to situations: all of these things contribute to the development of the teacher–student relationship, and help to define how their students feel about them.

The simple fact is, if students favour a teacher they are more likely to respond appropriately and behave cooperatively. It is not, however, a popularity contest. Being a favoured member of staff is not only about being a joker or 'young and trendy'. It is about giving and receiving respect, being fair but firm, showing students that you believe in them, but that you will not take any nonsense; ensuring that you know, and they know, what your expectations are. It helps if you have a sense of fun, but you also need to be regarded as a leader – a strong leader.

The intention of this section is to provide hints and ideas on how to establish and maintain meaningful, effective relationships with your students, how to communicate with them in respectful ways and provide positive leadership. Developing these skills will enhance your classroom experience and, importantly, have a significant impact on your efforts to successfully manage behaviour. Of course, everyone is an individual and brings their own unique qualities to the teaching profession; however, from within the variety there are a few key attributes that unite effective practitioners, and it is these that I will now discuss.

Be firm

Be firm: sounds obvious? Actually, it is not quite so straight-forward. It needs to be the right kind of firmness, delivered in the right kind of way – a way that is positive and conciliatory, as opposed to aggressive or divisive. I have watched many teachers dealing vigilantly with behaviour – they pick up on all the little problems, intervene quickly, and speak sharply – but never somehow penetrate through to the underlying motivations of their students. Behaviour does not improve, despite being persistently addressed: teachers that say all the right things, but say them in a cold, thin way that fails to make an impact. Delivery is everything.

Firm but encouraging
To tackle student behaviour with success, a teacher needs to project assertiveness and authority, but also warmth. A helpful way to achieve this is by using positive phrases that focus on what should be done rather than what shouldn't. 'You need to listen to what I am saying' is a lot more encouraging than 'Stop talking while I'm talking'. Your voice, though firm, should convey aspiration rather than frustration or irritation – a sense that the teacher actually cares and wants the child to behave. Effective teachers encourage their students to be more com-pliant by carefully implying that sticking to appropriate behaviour will be worth the effort, that the classroom experi-ence will be positive and enjoyable.

Focusing in
When effective teachers are being firm on problematic be-haviour, they zoom in on the situation. They emphatically engage with the student/group of students: speaking clearly and being specific, moving towards the problem and addressing individuals by name. Focus on quality of attention not quantity, ensuring that expectations are heard and understood. Try not to

confuse the issue by being vague or distant; and avoid layering the situation with any of your own underlying negative emotional agendas (boredom, annoyance, dislike, anger, power) – be straightforward, no-nonsense and direct.

Acting like you know what you are doing
Speak like you know what you want (even if you don't!), and stand like you are comfortable being up front (even if you're not!). Think of those staff members who have the ability to project authority into every corner of a room just by entering the doorway – kids rarely mess with them! If you can convey confidence and certainty, your students will feel instinctively obliged to respect you.

Think assertive
Of course, not everyone feels naturally sure of themselves. Experience helps, but even old hands can feel wary in the classroom. It is particularly tough if you are new to the profession – I have often wandered why assertiveness courses are not an essential part of the Initial Teacher Training curriculum. But it helps if you know what you want: before you meet your students, get your identity and expectations clear in your own mind. What are your intended outcomes for the lesson/project? What are you going to accept in terms of noise level, behaviour and attitude? What will you not accept, and how will you deal with this? Clarify what you want to achieve, picture yourself achieving it and focus on success.

Body language
It is possible to project a strong image (or fake it!) by simply paying attention to your body language. It is an issue of congruency – if your voice is trying to be firm, but your physicality suggests you are only half-interested or perhaps slightly intimidated, the impact of your approach will be significantly reduced.

1. Notice what you do with yourself while you teach: are you tense and self-conscious, or relaxed and open? Do you make large, elaborate hand gestures, or do you keep

your arms folded? Does your body language change according to the mood of the class?

2. Think about where you position yourself and how you position yourself. Are you confident standing out at the front, or do you feel more secure behind a desk – do what makes you feel most self-assured, but remember, the more omnipotent you are, the stronger your presence will be – place yourself where you can see and be seen.

3. Effective teachers are always on the move, and if a problem arises they appear – as if by magic – right next to it. Having said that, I once met a teacher who never came out from behind her desk (even during break times) but still managed to command 100 per cent attention – the fact that she had a stare like the Gorgon and a voice that sent tremors across the entire playground probably helped!

Physical gestures

Body language can often be used in place of the voice – just standing near to a student, folding your arms and looking bored when waiting for class attention can be enough to encourage a hush. A 'look' or a hand signal can be as effective as the spoken word. Such gestures can be consciously used to aid classroom control, but there are those that materialize without us knowing. I once observed a teacher who was having difficulties with a particular student. She explained that whenever she had to justifiably reprimand him for his restless behaviour, he would storm out of the room in an over-emotional, distressed state. I watched as she dealt with him and noticed that her approach towards him was menacing: shouting accompanied by aggressive finger pointing that almost took his eye out! A subsequent discussion revealed that she never realized she waggled her finger, let alone how threatening it seemed. If erratic gestures are a problem for you, try holding a pen – not only will it always be there when you need it, but it will assist you in controlling and making use of your body language. Having something in your hands forces you to be more conscious of what you do with them – your gestures will become more purposeful and emphatic.

Find your voice

Finding a special 'voice' for classroom control can be helpful. Effective teachers seem to slip into a particular tone when they are dealing with problematic behaviour or issuing instructions. It is a tone that is calm, focused and assertive, implying that the teacher is in control of the situation and is prepared to address the problem thoroughly (as opposed to impatiently trying to eliminate it). The teacher that has found their 'voice' rarely needs to shout or snap at their students; and if they do, it has greater impact (as it occurs so infrequently). Being able to confront behaviour without relying on constant shouting will preserve the vocal cords and also reduce the stress level within the classroom – beneficial to you and your students. Finding this voice and remembering to use it can take a bit of practice, but eventually it becomes an automatic response. For me personally, it is a matter of speaking 'lower and slower', which, in contrast to my usual excitable squeak, signals to my students that I now mean business!

Be prepared

One of the most common obstacles to feeling confident and firm in the classroom is anxiety about how to tackle very disruptive behaviour. There will be ideas and suggestions on how to cope with this issue throughout the book, but for now I will highlight one key part of the process: be prepared. It is not possible to predict exactly what will go on in a lesson, particularly if there are one or more difficult students in the class, but it is possible to feel more confidently prepared should difficulties arise. Behaviour management does not have to be imaginative or novel, in fact, it is most effective when it is repetitive and simple. Anticipate the sort of issues that may arise and how you intend to deal with them. Try to remember some stock phrases and consequences for possible problems, and then you can draw upon those should you feel lost.

Be fair

With so many pressures on today's teacher, it is tempting to seek the easiest solutions to classroom problems: the quicker a dispute can be solved, the quicker the lesson can get started. Any sniff of trouble from the serial lesson disrupter, send him to the deputy. Someone has scrawled an incorrectly spelt expletive on the whiteboard: it must be Gary because he is 'that' sort of boy (plus his literary skills are abysmal). Classrooms are busy places, and unfortunately you cannot always be in the right place at the right time – issues will arise without you realizing or fully understanding the cause. But if you do not take the trouble to ensure that a situation is resolved thoroughly and fairly, and if you rely on assumptions about individual behaviour, you risk losing the trust and respect of your students.

Being fair means being aware

Avoid making assumptions and automatically portioning blame even if an incident involves a known troublemaker. Certain students come with labels attached – lazy, rude, naughty, unpleasant, spiteful, disaffected – and it is all too easy to assume that they are somehow responsible for every mishap in the classroom. The spirit of 'innocent until proven guilty' can help you to avoid falling into this trap. This is not to suggest that difficult students should get away with their disruptive behaviour, but that it needs to be *their* behaviour.

1. Always investigate before persecuting individuals; allow students to explain their version of events and then pick the information apart.
2. Use phrases such as 'It looked as though ...' rather than direct accusations, and if you manage to get an admission, acknowledge it positively.
3. Unravelling the truth can be a tricky process. Sometimes it is evident that an individual has been responsible for a misdemeanour, however they will vehemently deny it or blame other people. Invite the student (as well as any others that may have been involved) to 'help' you get to the bottom of the problem.
4. Show that you are willing to be open-minded, but spell out the consequences of a) the incident itself, and b) dishonesty.
5. Emphasize that you respect honesty – the maturity and

courage it takes to come forward may lead to a more lenient sentence for those that do so!

Being fair is about showing some understanding

Students will struggle in class for many different reasons. If you are aware of any underlying factors – personal issues or family problems, for example – you may need to take this into account when considering how to deal with an individual. Is it helpful to have a go at them? Could you instead offer some support, have a quiet chat and show that you are sensitive to their situation? Explain that you are willing to make allowances, but that they need to do what they can to keep their behaviour in check/keep up with work/avoid confrontations. Offer some suggestions as to how you can help them: setting targets, giving discreet reminders (a nod, rather than a telling-off) or looking out for them. You can still lay down clear guidelines and expectations, but also show that you are prepared to be flexible. Letting a student know that you are on their side can have a very significant impact on their attitude to the classroom.

Being fair is a lesson in itself

If you adopt a balanced approach to dealing with disputes and conflicts, you are setting a good example to your students. You will be encouraging them to find well-rounded and rational resolutions, which may help them to solve conflicts in the world beyond school. Always give students an opportunity to express themselves and put forward their side of the story, in turn and without interruptions, whether they are the guilty party, the victim or the antagonist. Encourage them to do this in a calm, mature manner – listening to one another and respecting each person's point of view. Help them to develop their own discussions about how to move the situation forward. Okay, so it takes time and effort to do this, time away from learning the curriculum – but in doing it you are teaching young people valuable communication skills, skills that have as much (if not more) relevance in modern life as a formal education does.

Being fair means issuing fair sanctions

Having a system of rewards and consequences can be a useful tool for managing classroom behaviour. It is important, however, that they are used judiciously. When it comes to rewards, it is important to recognize that some students will never be able to meet the standards of behaviour and work that are achieved by the majority of the class – but they still need incentives. Make sure that you identify the effort and achievement of individuals in relation to themselves – even if you find yourself giving merit to a child that has finally remembered his pencil case (insignificant to others, but a giant leap of progress for him!). With consequences, it is important to remember the rationale behind them. They should be issued as a way of helping the student to learn from their mistakes and make amends for their misdemeanours, as opposed to 'punishment' or pure cold-blooded teacher revenge...

Be calm

A calm teacher's presence is instantly recognizable. The atmosphere in their classroom is peaceful, the noise level stays generally low and communication between individuals is polite and respectful. The teacher is able to keep students on track without raising his/her voice or sounding annoyed, and students respond quickly to any instructions or reminders. If this is the kind of classroom environment you aspire to, remember, none of it happens by accident. The teacher in question makes ongoing endeavours to establish and maintain a calm, stable atmosphere.

Seemingly effortless classroom control relies on a lot of background work: much of it relating to keeping a grip on your own feelings and responses to the pressures of the classroom. Feeling impatient, angry or irritated by certain students/situations is only human; but the master of the craft is able to conceal these emotions and replace them with controlled assertiveness (at least until they reach the sanctuary of the staff room!).

The benefits of being calm in the classroom are bountiful. If you present yourself as a generally even-natured individual, this will set a precedent for the overall classroom atmosphere. If a classroom is managed in a way that is erratic and unpredictable – the teacher switching between moods, from impatience to hostility to annoyance – students may become increasingly irritable and distracted. But if the classroom is calm, so too are the students, resulting in fewer incidents of stressful behaviour.

When dealing with specific difficulties, adopting a calm approach can make a significant difference to the outcome of the situation. If a student is seeking to disrupt the class or cause conflict, any expression of hostility, aggression, ridicule or frustration is likely to inflame the problem rather than diffuse it. If the student is handled with a calm, measured approach, their own unsettled mood may be soothed and neutralized.

Just to clarify for all the sceptics out there, I mean *calm*, not 'soft'. It is not about being gentle and fluffy, it is simply about being in control of your own voice and emotions. You can still be firm and 'no nonsense' but the secret is doing this without projecting unsettling emotional ambiguity. Negative or unpredictable emotional undertones, unless your students know and trust you well, will work against you. To them, sudden stroppy outbursts may imply that you lack self-control, that you are easily wound-up (light entertainment for some) or that you are a threat – seeking 'power' over your students.

I have frequently, and painfully, observed teachers trying to deal with problematic students by locking into argument, determined to show their ability to retain dominance by becoming increasingly louder and angrier – resulting in per-sonal insults and verbal aggression. Rising to conflict, however frustrated you feel, only makes a situation worse. Stay calm. Separate your key objective (to diffuse the problem) from your emotional feelings about the behaviour; and separate your reaction to the behaviour from your reaction to the student (in other words, don't get personal). Some may argue that if a student misbehaves they deserve to be made to feel bad, but this is a defeatist way of looking at it: focusing on revenge rather than progress.

Be consistent

One of the quickest ways to lose your grasp on a class is to deal with their behaviour inconsistently. Teachers often come to me complaining that, although they had a good initial relationship with a certain class or group of students, they can no longer get them to listen or settle. After a bit if investigative work, it often comes to light that the teacher has been a bit 'hit or miss' with their boundary keeping: sometimes they can be bothered to get students to remove their caps and jackets, sometimes it's more hassle than it's worth. Sometimes a student may get sent out for swearing, sometimes it's all just a laugh. If your students think there is any chance that they can get away with something, they may as well try – and they can always throw it right back at you if you try to clamp down: '. . . but you didn't tell Sandra off last week! That's not fair! I'm not listening to you anymore.'

Consistency enables you to establish a reliable, respectable identity among your students. Having this identity will enhance your ability to manage their behaviour and coerce their cooperation. Being consistent is helpful in a number of ways:

- It makes a clear, strong statement about the fact that you are not someone who will tolerate unacceptable behaviour: that there will be follow-up.
- It implies that you are rational, dependable and fair: someone that students can trust.
- It helps students to familiarize themselves with the boundaries of acceptable behaviour, minimizing opportunities for them to make excuses or feign ignorance.
- It enables students to understand what is expected of them in terms of work output and conduct.
- It reduces the risk of students claiming, rightly or wrongly, that they have been treated unfairly – which leads to resentment and dispute.
- Within the wider environment, it helps to define the ethos of a school and consolidate behaviour management – it shows that teachers work as a team, will deal with things as a team, and are therefore closed to any attempts to be manipulated or avoided.

Being consistent, however, can feel like hard work. If you are tired, or simply not in the mood, it is tempting to just let things slip past you quietly; but if you can get it right for the majority of the time, your classroom life will become easier. It pays to start straight away. Establish a process of clarifying your expectations and dealing with challenging behaviour as soon as you start working with a new class. There is a well-known cliché in education: don't smile until Christmas. To me, it is not about being nasty or scary, it is about not letting up. Do not let up on your behaviour management campaign until your class instinctively know what you want from them. You may find you are dealing with the same sorts of issues every lesson, however, if you persist and are consistent in your approach – your class WILL get the message, and the bulk of the remaining year will be much more peaceful as a result.

Be positive

Being positive is about creating an atmosphere, making your class into a place that you and your students would like to be in. If students feel welcome, if they feel comfortable about being in the classroom, they will be in a much better position to engage with their work and with you. In order for them to feel this way, they need to be encouraged and supported, regardless of their ability or their attitude. Being positive will also be beneficial to you: drawing attention to good behaviour can help you to focus on the more rewarding aspects of the job, and therefore make you feel less stressed.

I was once asked to observe a 'problem' class in a primary school. The teacher warned me that they were a really difficult bunch, and that challenging behaviour had reached new lows – he was at his wits' end. Sure enough, I found the atmosphere of that class to be very negative, but it was immediately evident that much of this negativity was emanating from the teacher himself. He was so stressed out that he could do little to hide the fact that he was losing the will. His behaviour management had become a desperate stream of angry shouting; when he wasn't shouting he sat with his head in his hands. He had no faith in the class, and they knew it. However, as an outside observer, I noticed that there were several times during the day when the class were actually working well – they were on task and quiet. There was also an incident in which one of the most difficult students, on his own initiative, did something really helpful for the teacher. All of these things passed unnoticed.

My advice to that teacher (besides take a week off!) was: make a conscious effort to notice and praise the right kind of behaviour – even if you can only find minor things. Sometimes it is difficult to see beyond the frustration that a difficult class or student can create, but everyone needs encouragement. Acknowledging improvements, successes or effort – if necessary, regarding minor things – can make a considerable difference. Show them that you at least believe they will eventually get it right, even if they are a long way off.

When disciplining an individual, it is helpful to end with some positive reinforcement: a comment or reminder that, despite the difficulty, you still wish for the child to succeed and be part of the classroom. This is not always easy: you may be fed up of persistent difficult behaviour or an unpleasant attitude, but things will not improve if you do not create the potential for them to improve. A significant amount of disruptive behaviour is the result of low self-esteem – sad rather than bad.

Confronting a student about their behaviour actually provides a good opportunity to instill positive comments about them – at a time when they are perhaps feeling reflective and self-aware. Use this opportunity. Remind them of what they are capable of, what they can achieve, of their successes – steer them away from a negative spiral.

2 Styles to avoid . . .

Teaching style is a personal issue. The aforementioned qualities (firm, fair, calm, consistent and positive), though the backbone of successful classroom practice, are by no means the sum total of a teacher's style and charisma. It is sometimes surprising to see how certain members of staff relate to their students: the tiny, timid woman that never speaks to anyone in the staffroom, but can get the rowdiest class quiet in seconds; the eccentric design and technology teacher who dresses like a lunatic, but is adored by the most hardened 15 year olds! There are no hard and fast rules. Some staff will make a conscious decision to project a certain image; others will just be themselves.

While it can be difficult to pinpoint what makes for effective teacher charisma – for I have seen such a strange variety of flair and personality out there – it is easy to identify some of the approaches that are commonly problematic. The following descriptions are intended to provide a light-hearted illumination of these teaching personality clichés. They are problematic because they lead to student resentment (although some members of the profession may not view that as such a bad thing!).

The dragon

Every school has one. And they have a valuable role to play: the one all the students are scared of. Usually the 'dragon' occupies a senior management position, having been sourced for their extraordinary ability to make the lips of the toughest quiver with fear. All well and good, but if you are a 'heavy' in training – i.e., you do not have an office with Deputy Head on the door yet – you still have some classroom teaching to do! Being strict does, of course, carry benefits.

- Firm discipline: students will have a clear sense of class-room behaviour boundaries, and will be more cautious about crossing them.
- The 'snow-ball' effect of a strong reputation: new students will be wary of messing a known authoritarian about.
- Quieter lessons: a tightly controlled classroom environment can be an easier place to work in, facilitating academic focus and progress.

Being *ultra* strict, however, can have negative consequences. Having a firm grasp on your students is one thing, intimidating them is another. Fortunately, I have only seen a small number of teachers cross this line – but it is a line that needs to be respected. Are your students cooperating with you because they respect you, or because they are frightened of you? Do you encourage them to do the 'right' thing, or do you bully them into submission? Do you teach them to be responsible for themselves, or do you do their thinking for them?

The main casualties of an ultra-strict teacher are often the most vulnerable: the students that struggle with self-esteem or lack confidence in the classroom, perhaps because of learning, emotional or behavioural issues. These students may struggle to keep up with everyone else, and they may find it difficult to keep their behaviour in check – especially if the person ordering them about is making them feel anxious or useless. In my experience, ultra-strict teachers will use 'carrots' (such as praise) very sparingly, making it hard for students with low self-esteem to feel secure and motivated.

I can recall being invited to watch 'The Secret Weapon' in practice: a primary school teacher whose extreme strictness was apparently very impressive. Indeed it was impressive – I had never seen such a quiet group of 9 year olds. But I was also aware of a disarmingly cold, oppressive atmosphere that seemed to hold the classroom to ransom. The students had very nervous facial expressions and seemed frightened to contribute to class discussion. Students were not allowed to talk, move, look away momentarily or ask each other for help. Individuals that did not offer to answer questions during the teacher-led session were criticized for being lazy – I cannot help thinking their reluctance had more to do with the fact that any student getting an answer wrong or only partially right was sharply and unpleasantly told they hadn't been listening properly. I would rather see a group of rowdy, excitable individuals clambering to express themselves, than to have to witness those fearful, anxiety-stricken faces ever again!

The mouse

Some teachers have mastered the art of having a low-key presence in the classroom. They are able to operate in a quiet but dynamic way, using patience, calmness and poise to great effect. The secret is emotional tension: serenity spring-loaded with underlying firmness. Students will relate to the gentle presence of this kind of teacher, but will be distinctly aware of something powerful within! A sense that this member of staff will know exactly what to do if anyone misbehaves. There are some teachers, however, that have a low-key presence in the classroom, without any of this skill – in other words 'weak'.

The weak teacher, or as I have suggested, the 'mouse', is the sort of teacher who squeaks beneath the din of the mob, whose classroom is run by the students. Perhaps everyone has had an experience of a class that is particularly difficult to manage, or that they feel intimidated by; but the 'mouse' struggles to manage the top set. They rely on small, monotone requests for cooperation, and when that fails to work, they beg! They do not relate to their students or make bold decisions (like rethinking a seating plan); they are afraid to challenge rule breaking, or to enforce routines – in short, they allow the students to dictate the expectations and atmosphere of the classroom. They earn themselves a reputation as a 'do whatever you like' teacher, which does not help the cause. And unfortunately, failing to get a grip on classroom management may mean failing to get a grip on student learning – the two go hand in hand.

While I feel some sympathy for those who struggle to make a forceful impact in the classroom, it is of curiosity to me that some of them choose to remain in the profession. I make this point because many of the weak teachers I have come across are not necessarily new to the experience – they have been doing it for some time, putting up with the same student mutiny for years, as though it is perfectly acceptable. If the skills required to manage a classroom sufficiently (let alone efficiently) are not a) coming to them naturally, or b) being picked up along the way, then perhaps teaching is simply not their calling!

The pupil's 'friend'

Arrgghh! There is nothing more annoying than the staff member who thinks they can curry favour with their students by getting 'in' with them. We all appreciate getting on with our classes: positive interaction fosters a productive working environment and makes the day more agreeable for everyone. But it is too easy, especially if you are new to the profession (and I know I was once guilty of this), to mislead yourself into thinking that being 'liked' at all costs by your students will make you invincible. Do not be fooled...

Watching the teacher who lives up to the 'pupil's friend' stereotype is like watching an ITV sitcom – there's something slightly desperate about it. The fan club, the doting 12-year-old girls, the high-fives in the corridor – all those trappings of popularity. Yes it may seem tantalizing at first, but it will all turn sour when exams come round. Too many hours spent chatting about Sir's round-the-world backpacking adventure mean vital chunks of the curriculum have been skipped – and try forcing coursework out of a girl who regards you as one of her 'mates': 'Aw, gimme a break, Sir – you used to be a laugh. What's up with you?'

Putting popularity before solid classroom practice causes confusion for the impressionable students that fall for it; but others will be more sceptical. The simple fact is most students are not looking for another friend (hopefully, they'll have plenty of those – of their own age); they are looking for someone who can control the group, who can fulfil the leader role – someone who will guide them through the day/lesson, making them feel safe, secure and accounted for. They understand what the teacher's role is for – they will like you enough if you take on this role with respect and enthusiasm. They do not need to be wooed.

There is a difference between being popular and being respected – effective teachers achieve a balance of both. Being someone the students can relate to, having a sense of humour, dropping in comments about subject matter you know will appeal to their youthfulness – these things are certainly helpful; but they are only a tiny part of what makes a student respect you. They also need to trust you, believe that you care about them, feel motivated by you, know that you will deal with unacceptable behaviour and know that you will stop them when they go too far. Many teachers manage to balance the popularity game with clearly defined classroom/learning expectations, but their success depends on having the strength to be firm on discipline, knowing how and when to pull the class in. Successful teachers always retain a little bit of distance between themselves and their students.

The foe

People often assume that because I work in schools I love children: all children, anyone's children – I don't! I am fascinated by them and I enjoy working with them – but I don't love them *per se*. It was the most frightening moment of my life when one of my more problematic students mistakenly called me 'Mummy'! To make the most of the profession you do not need to be an outright youth enthusiast, but you do need to accept the fact that you will spend entire days surrounded by hundreds of them.

Occasionally I come across teachers who seem to actively hate young people – or at least the amount of moaning they do leads me to think so. While letting rip in the sanctuary of the staffroom has many stress-soothing benefits, there are those that do it habitually – in fact, they never seem to have anything positive to say about the students or the job.

'So-and-so has been an evil little **** today hasn't he? As always...'
'9G are the most useless bunch of idiots I've ever met – what's the point – none of them will get any GCSEs anyway...'

If it makes you that miserable – go and do something else! The 'foe' is the type of teacher that sees the student as the enemy, as a joyless entity that needs to be resented. The general implication is that students are an inconvenience, or that the sole purpose of their actions is simply to cause problems. The foe's preferred method of classroom control is regular criticism, and they tend to hold grudges. Unfortunately for the foe, their manner in turn does little to encourage their students to be charming and sweet. What is the point in being polite to people that seem to dislike you whatever you do? The atmosphere is dictated by negativity – not a good environment for fostering enthusiasm for education.

The uncommitted

What do artists, writers, musicians, actors, scientists, historians or those of an academic persuasion do when they find they are struggling to make a living? Teach. Some of them find happiness in the classroom; some of them do not quite find happiness, but feel comfortably satisfied; and some of them spend their school careers dwelling on what could have been, had they not 'sold out' to education. Teaching is a job that needs commitment. Its demands are intense, but if these demands can be tackled with stamina and enthusiasm, it can be an enjoyable, rewarding career. The problem is, if you are one of those individuals who spends their classroom life wishing they were somewhere else, doing something else, it can be hard to find the required motivation.

Everyone has times when they would rather be with their families, on a yacht or back in bed – than at work. It is when that feeling takes over, when you find yourself constantly wishing you could be *anywhere* other than in the classroom that you should start to question your situation. Uncharacteristically dreading going to work is a sign of stress, which will need to be addressed – time for a change, time for a break, time to ask for support? Temporary loss of commitment or interest in the job can be overcome, and besides, the world will not collapse if you occasionally fail to get your marking done on time.

The 'uncommitted' teacher, however, is the one who lacks

enthusiasm for the job from the moment they embark on their training. They do not view teaching as a profession, they view at as a means to an end: a way of making a stable income. But to the true believers teaching is neither of those things – it is a way of life! Unless these views can be reconciled, the journey may be long and painful. Half-heartedness is unhealthy for the teacher, who will constantly battle with piles of unmarked coursework, unplanned lessons and the consequences of lazy behaviour management. But it is unhealthy for the student too: they will miss out in many ways if their teacher is too bored to give them a quality learning experience.

3 Talents you never knew you had . . .

So you've made it through the hurdles of 'Styles to avoid . . .'. You neither beg, bully nor bumble your way through classroom control – you are a *good* teacher! Just to massage your ego further, here is a reminder of some of the many, many talents that the teaching profession can draw out of you.

Entertaining

Yes, the main aim is to impart knowledge and wisdom, but gone are the days of blackboards, chalk and lists of facts. With such stiff competition, in the form of television, computer games and . . . more computer games, teachers everywhere find themselves drawing on their resourcefulness; seeking new and exciting ways of engaging student interest; proving that subordinate clauses *are* more exciting than 'Zombie Smash III'. There are those that are able to entertain effortlessly – they only need to open their mouths and something witty leaps out. Some relish the idea of performance, delivering their lessons with enthusiasm and energy – using their sparkle to illuminate the most boring mathematical equation. But for those who are not so comically or charismatically blessed, there is also a range of tried-and-tested techniques that do not require joke-telling, juggling, acrobatics or any other uncomfortable form of self-promotion:

- Visual resources
- Relating subject matter to students' own lives
- Kinaesthetic activities
- Role-play
- Debate
- Demonstrations/introductions that surprise or shock.

These techniques will be discussed in greater detail in the following chapter ('Making it Interesting', p. 31), but rest assured they are reliable and effective, and can be applied (with just a little imagination) to any subject. It is a myth that some subjects are, by their natures, more interesting than others – I am fascinated by history (a subject that beautifully lends itself to imaginative teaching), but sat through enough lifeless history classes during my youth to decide to give it up at the earliest opportunity. The facts don't always speak for themselves – it is how we present them.

Conflict resolving

Schools operate like little communities, and within any community we can expect conflict to arise from time to time. As teachers we are the gatekeepers and guardians of these communities, and therefore have a role to play in keeping the peasants (our students) in order. Although it can sometimes feel like a waste of precious time and frustration, the social politics and disputes that emerge between students are a valuable part of school education, of discovering how to be part of a community. Situations such as arguments are rich in opportunities for learning about problem solving and communication: skills that are necessary for life, but not necessarily discovered in life … unless they are taught.

Although it is difficult to escape from the mountain of demands that the conventional curriculum places on the teacher, it is sometimes worth stepping back and remembering that school is about so much more than a list of attainment targets and assessment levels (for the students, at least). Learning how to function socially is just as significant as learning the multiplication table – and teachers can play a valuable role in promoting this learning: encouraging students to communicate effectively, to treat each other respectfully and to develop ways of solving conflict that do not result in resentment, violence or bullying. Although much of this work will be done indirectly, with good teachers establishing a general atmosphere of positivity, it is sometimes helpful to teach through example: next time your meticulously prepared lesson on binary numbers is dominated by an intense and vicious girl-fight, think 'social skills learning opportunity'!

Delegating

Teachers are often thought of as single operators, captains of their own ships. This idea of independence appeals to many, but with so much to be responsible for it can sometimes feel overwhelming. The solution: delegate. Although it is a term more commonly associated with the business world, delegation is just as applicable to the classroom teacher, though the expectations are often less formal – a team leader asks her staff for a report on the latest company figures, and it is on her desk by noon. A curriculum coordinator asks his staff for a copy of their timetables, and he is told to get stuffed!

Schools have a rich supply of people that are willing and able to ease some of the teacher's burden: support assistants, caretakers, secretaries, subject technicians and librarians to name but a few. Even the students themselves can be useful oil for the classroom machinery. As an ex-art teacher, I know full well the value of getting students to take responsibility for organizing and tidying up the classroom: sink monitor, brush monitor, paint palette monitor, paper monitor and even picking-the-scraps-of-dried-clay-from-the-floor monitor – all had their function and focus. On good days it was as efficient as a beehive, on bad days it resembled the ensemble at a bad circus – but at least I was never left alone to deal with a sink full of gunk (most of it was on the children!).

Delegation is supposed to make your life easier: distribute the tasks you can trust to others, and liberate some of your time to focus on other responsibilities. But delegation can be a task in itself: knowing how to get what you want and who to get it from is vitally important. Learn to give explicit instructions, seek out reliable people and always express gratitude. And finally, never assume that because you like things 'just-so', other people will have the same approach. There is nothing more frustrating than having to chase-up and, in the last minute, re-do the work that someone else was supposed to have completed. Check in advance. Is the photocopying you asked for being stapled correctly? Has the register found its way back to the school office? Why has the class hamster become so thin?

Inspiring

Many would agree that one of the most appealing, rewarding aspects of the teaching profession is watching young people grow and develop, as a direct result of what you, their teacher, have provided for them. You are contributing to their life. It is a daunting responsibility, but also incredibly exciting. And it is not just the inspired nuggets of golden learning that leave an impression on your students. They are looking at your personality, your attitude to life, your enthusiasm and your way of making them feel important ... If anyone complains that modern living makes them feel insignificant and unable to influence the state of the world, tell them to become a teacher – schools are full of opportunities to create change.

Some of the recent British adverts promoting careers in education are reminding us that teachers have an inspirational quality about them. But the question is ... do their students realize they have this inspirational quality? The reality: for all those students that are going to have their lives shaped and influenced by their wonderful teachers, there will be just as many who shuffle from classroom to classroom without being stirred by a single word (until eventually they shuffle right out of the school gates, and spend the rest of their education smoking fags behind the chippy). So perhaps the biggest task when it comes to inspiring, is finding a way to make education meaningful to everyone. How can we make the experience of school touch the most disaffected, disillusioned and disassociated? How can we get them to take pride in learning if they simply do not see the value of it?

Empathizing

Learning to see the world through someone else's eyes can have an enormous impact on every teacher. Having a sense of what makes young people tick, however peculiar, irritating or difficult they are, enables us to step back and understand. Empathy gives us the capacity to tolerate different behaviours and different attitudes. Being able to recognize and accept the reasons why an individual may be acting the way they are allows us to exercise control over our own reactions. Although we may choose to show our disapproval of certain behaviour, if we have an understanding of why it may be occurring, we are less likely to take it personally. If we are not taking it personally, we can approach the matter in a more rational way: which is better for everyone involved.

Empathy with younger children and then teenagers involves different modes of thinking, but the real challenge is empathizing with disruptive, disturbed individuals, whatever age they are. If these are the students that give you the biggest headache, empathy will at least ease the pressure of thinking they are deliberately trying to make your life hell. Consider what bothers you about their behaviour: they waste so much time, they are rude to you, they disturb the rest of the class, they stop you from doing your job . . . and then think carefully about what they might be trying to achieve: getting attention (do they feel unimportant?), avoiding a task in order to not fail it (do they have low self-esteem?) or trying to prove themselves to the rest of the class (are they insecure?).

Part 2

Lesson Structure and Content

4 Keeping them motivated . . .

I am often asked to observe teachers who feel they are struggling with their behaviour-management skills, only to find that their skills are pretty good. What they are struggling with, and the reason why they are experiencing problems with challenging behaviour, is the structure and content of their actual teaching. Individuals, or even whole classes, will quickly lose interest in a lesson (and therefore resort to less desirable ways of entertaining themselves) if the learning opportunities, for various reasons, are not drawing them in. Maybe the delivery is uninteresting, the subject matter confusing, or the information simply not accessible: too difficult, or too irrelevant. Every teacher, at some point, has delivered the kind of lesson that has had all their students captivated for the entire duration – what was the secret? Okay, so it was Christmas word searches. But in truth, everyone's attention can be grabbed and harnessed somehow. The challenge is knowing what buttons to press. Fortunately there are a variety of solutions to the problem – some simple, some not so simple. As with all things in teaching, planning ahead and being prepared is the easiest way to get on top of the learning process in the classroom, and will enable you to make (almost) every lesson dynamic, progressive and accessible to all.

Providing a challenge

The level of challenge can be tricky to get right. Too little, and your students will feel bored, patronized and de-motivated. Too much, and they may well feel frightened, insecure and, again, de-motivated. Add to this the fact that many classes are made up of students with varied levels of ability, and will often have a handful of students with particular learning needs. Here are some suggestions on how to provide effective challenge:

Discover for yourself

It is always worth investing some time, early in the year, on assessing your students' capabilities and checking what they already know. SATs results and level indicators are helpful but do not necessarily give the practical and specific information you need for getting to grips with individual strengths, weaknesses and learning styles. Set some straightforward tasks that will help you to check what they know (never assume) and assess where they are at within different aspects of the subject – use this information to inform your future planning.

Plan for progress

When putting together worksheets or tasks, think in terms of easy/medium/hard. Hopefully, the majority of your students will fall broadly into these categories – some will be able to progress through each level, others will stick where they are at for longer. Providing two or three different levels of work need not be too onerous: take the same task or set of questions and simplify/complicate them as necessary. If you have a few bright sparks in your class, try to keep a bank of additional/extension tasks at the ready. If you have students with particularly low attainment, make sure that tasks are simple enough so they can at least attempt to complete them independently.

Praise and encourage

Whatever level your students are working at, they will all benefit from praise and encouragement. Likewise, they may sometimes need reassurance when tackling new challenges or unfamiliar topics. If it is taking a while for them to grasp something, remind them not to worry – encourage and support their efforts as much as their achievements.

Ask them

When trying to pitch work at the right level, it is sometimes helpful to seek the student's opinion. Not only can this provide a useful indicator of their levels of confidence and ability, but it will also help to make them feel included in the organization of their learning. Encourage students to reflect on their achievements and consider for themselves what they have struggled and succeeded with; having some ownership over learning can improve motivation.

Push them

If a class is challenging in terms of behaviour, it is easy to become wary of pushing them too hard academically – the fear of students not coping with the work and therefore playing up, or a lost cause ('... none of them care about their exams anyway'). But remember, work that is too easy, or lacks challenge, can be just as potent a recipe for misbehaviour. Focus on progression, no matter how slow, therefore there will always be an appropriate challenge on the horizon. Consistently show them that you have high (albeit reasonable) expectations of their potential, and they may start to believe you.

Making it interesting

Lessons can be brought to life in a variety of ways, without necessarily requiring a lot of extra effort on your part. Simple additions or adaptations can make a huge difference, and will enable you to cater for different learning styles by prompting different sensory faculties into action.

Using visual resources

Images and artefacts are a simple but effective way to bring a subject to life. Whether it is an English lesson about *Macbeth* (photographs of the murky Highlands, or film/theatre images of different character portrayals), or a chemistry lesson about the Periodic Table (examples of different substances and materials that can be handled and examined close up), the inclusion of relevant visual material can be the hook that pulls students in. With the dawn of the Internet, accessing relevant images has become quite straightforward; and many libraries/museums are willing to loan boxes of artefacts for a variety topics – stuffed animals, periodic costume, masks from different cultures, you name it.

Making subject matter relevant

If the student will not come to the knowledge, bring the knowledge to the student! Emphasize comparisons between their lives and the lives of the people and characters representing whichever period of history, area of the world, book, play or culture being studied. If students are encouraged to interpret information in the context of their own experiences, they will have a greater chance of connecting with it. In certain instances, it is helpful to show students how certain skills and knowledge will be applicable to their own futures: being able to handle money, using verbal reasoning to get their own way, writing a mind-blowing job application. We know how important education is – we somehow need to show them!

Kinaesthetic activities

Activities that involve movement or physical engagement with information can be an effective way to refresh learning. It can be as simple as asking students to respond to questions by moving to 'yes/no/maybe' sections of space, or it could be an elaborately thought out interactive trail of discovery. There is always an element of fun attached to being able to move around and 'do', and although this may require some hawk-like attention to behaviour management, such adventure can often lead to an invigorating, memorable experience. Kinaesthetic activity can transform the most mundane of learning exercises into game-like enjoyment, for example, 'mathematical catch': a quick-fire round of questions starting with the teacher. Ask a question, throw a small ball at the person you wish to answer it – if they catch the ball and answer correctly, they repeat the process for someone else. The aim is to get round everyone without dropping the ball or answering incorrectly.

Speaking and listening activities

Tasks such as role-play or debate can be fruitful in terms of encouraging students to engage with a subject and formulate opinions. As a less structured way of exploring a topic, debate allows students to take some ownership of what is being discussed, and sometimes encourages quieter or less enthusiastic class members to contribute. It is also an excellent way for developing effective communication skills. Role-play can be used in a variety of ways, encouraging students to think laterally and engage with ideas. On a simple level, I have often asked my own students to role-play 'being the teacher' – which they always relish! I invite one of them to stand at the whiteboard and explain a topical maths question or science idea to me as if I was the student. It is an amusingly effective way of encouraging them to make solid sense of their own knowledge and understanding.

Demonstrations that surprise or shock
Grab their attention in the first instance, and they will forever look out for you to do the next wacky thing – hence they might listen and look a bit more carefully!

Trips, visits and speakers
Although these things may require some effort in terms of organization, the results can often be worth it. Leaving the four walls of the classroom can invigorate and excite the minds of your students – and not just because they do not have to wear uniform for a day/get to sit next to each other on the bus/spend their money in the gift shop. Carefully chosen trips can ignite interest in a particular topic or subject. If trips feel like too much risk or responsibility, asking a guest speaker to come to the classroom can be an equally effective way of bringing the class to life – a war veteran, a local journalist, someone's mum (who happens to be related to Nelson Mandela) or even a teacher from another department!

Differentiation

Catering for every individual student's learning needs is never an easy task, especially in secondary education, where teachers have limited time to familiarize themselves with each individual. I have frequently seen the negative consequences of a student struggling in a class where the work is clearly unsuitable for them. What happens? They become agitated and despondent, they give up, they mess about to distract from their failure and they get sent out of the classroom.

Despite the rigours of the literacy and numeracy programmes, there will always be students who have significant difficulty coping with basic skills. Although the development of small withdrawal groups can improve progress, lack of these skills (especially in literacy) will interfere with a student's access to all areas of the curriculum: differentiation should be accounted for in every subject. Students with particularly poor literacy, for instance, may have difficulties simply reading instructions on a worksheet.

The art of differentiation is to make the subject matter accessible to everyone, and in an ideal world this would be done without patronizing or humiliating low achievers. However it can be difficult to set tasks for low-ability students, without some of them resenting the fact that they are getting the 'baby' work. Soothe their egos by avoiding singling students out or drawing attention to their differences, and explain that everyone in the class is working at a different level – not just them.

Be wary of underestimating your students, but also of overestimating: they will not necessarily tell you that they are unable to read the text, use complete sentences, or understand the question. I will now offer some general tips for tackling low literacy that can be applied to any subject. Low literacy skills can mean students will struggle to:

- cope with large amounts of independent writing;
- read or follow instructions/text independently;
- absorb, retain and process information;
- work at a rate equitable with the rest of the class.

Differentiation is not just about adjusting tasks, but also about adjusting expectations. You will know what you want the majority of your students to achieve by the end of a lesson or project, think too about what you want the less able individuals to achieve – they may not be able to understand the form and function of several types of animal cell, but they may be able to recognize and label a simple diagram. Set goals that are appropriate for them.

Decide what the purpose of the task is: are you looking for a demonstration of knowledge and understanding, or the development of written work and presentation? Where understanding is important, is it really necessary for the student to produce pages of writing, when the task of writing itself my baffle and overwhelm them? There are many alternative ways to aid and test a student's understanding of a concept.

- Close procedure exercises (filling in the blanks): which encourage students to recognize and understand key vocabulary in context, while minimizing the need to write (but they will need to read).
- Sequencing activities: tasks that involve organizing information (either written or image based) into appropriate order, for example, the order in which a science experiment was carried out, or historical event took place.
- Worksheets that involve cutting, sticking and labelling pieces of information.
- Group work involving verbal discussion of ideas rather than writing, or perhaps using a more able student as the scribe.
- Asking students to produce a diagram/artistic representation of their understanding of a piece of information (particularly effective when looking at descriptive writing).

If expressing ideas in written form is the key objective of a task, then there are several ways of making this easier for the student that struggles to write independently.

- Provide key vocabulary lists (either on the board or as a separate handout).
- Provide word banks (lists of spellings for frequently used words).
- Provide photocopied guidelines or wide ruled paper/ exercise books for students who have difficulties with handwriting.
- Provide photocopied writing frameworks (available form the Internet/literacy resource books) to help with planning, structure and organization of written work – there is

nothing more off-putting to a reluctant writer than a huge blank page.

- Provide a selection of written questions/phrases that can act as prompts for enabling the student to formulate ideas, or remember what information to include.
- Give specific guidance on how much you expect the student to write (and remember to adjust your expectations accordingly). Two pages? Three paragraphs? Five sentences?
- Where suitable, allow access to a computer – this can make a huge difference to a student's motivation.

Setting targets

Targets can be set for a variety of reasons, but in terms of motivating students they prompt and clarify what needs to be done, and define what has been achieved: think of how satisfying it is to tick off items on a 'to do' list! Having clear markers of success helps to illuminate the progress that is being made. This is important for all students, but is particularly valuable in terms of motivating those that have low self-esteem. It is simply not possible to set and review specific targets for every individual student, at every step of the way, but there will be certain individuals who may really benefit form this kind of personalized input. Others may be suitably able to motivate and set goals for themselves.

Targets can be used for groups of students, the whole class, or individuals; but whomever they apply to, their effectiveness relies on several key features. Helpful targets are meaningful, achievable, specific, measurable and time restricted.

Meaningful

Telling a child you want to hear them contributing more frequently to class discussion is not a target; it is a comment. Targets need to be set and then used emphatically. When setting whole-class targets, make a display out of them; for individuals, write targets in their exercise books (on the page they will be looking at), or have them typed and stuck on desks (if appropriate). Remind and encourage students about what they are aiming for.

Achievable

Perhaps this goes without saying! The idea of targets is that they encourage success, not intimidate or demoralize – make sure they are realistic, and that the students view them as realistic. For this reason, it is sometimes more helpful to set individual targets instead of/as well as whole-class ones: Jonny may be able to learn five CVC words in a week, but the likelihood of him getting to grips with 'iambic pentameter' is pretty slim...

Specific

Targets need to be clear and concrete, written in language that is understandable to the student. It is far more effective to focus on small details of achievement, than on general ideas, which can sometimes be open to interpretation. For example, 'use capital letters at the start of each new sentence', is more purposeful than 'improve punctuation'.

Measurable

Each target needs to be something both you and your student can recognize has been done, and that will yield evidence of success. The criteria for this can be set out in the target itself, for example, 'to answer 8/10 multiplication questions correctly in next week's test'. Trying to meet that challenge will make it a more tangible, and perhaps fun, experience.

Time restricted

If we had endless time to achieve our goals, how hard would we actually work? Targets need to be attached to time restraints, whether they are half a term, the duration of a project or during the next written task. If they are not achieved within that time, they can always be reviewed and revisited.

Pacing tasks

Pacing a lesson is extremely important: there is a well-known notion that 20 minutes is the limit of the average adult's concentration span (less for younger people). From my own classroom observations, it seems those who act on this point are able to draw every last drop from their students. Their lessons tend to be broken down into smaller sections, so that several tasks of differing natures can take place in any one session: energetic, varied and busy. Watching the teacher that chooses to plod through an hour or more with one monotonous activity, particularly if it involves listening, can be very disheartening, especially when the teacher starts to shout at the students for failing to pay attention: why is Gary drawing marijuana leaves all over his exercise book? Because he is bored witless!

Bringing pace and variety into your lessons can be a demanding exercise, as it requires more organization and 'pizazz' from you. Those that rise to the challenge, however, will undoubtedly profess that the benefits outweigh the additional effort. Sustaining student interest by providing a variety of shorter tasks can help to minimize boredom and off-task behaviour. It also means that students can stay focused for longer periods of time, therefore maximizing learning opportunities.

Below are some suggestions for how to pace your lessons effectively.

Younger students need fairly rapid task progression (15 to 20 minutes being the maximum time spent on any one focused activity); older students are able to sustain a reasonable level of interest for longer periods, but considering some lessons will last for up to two hours, opportunities for refreshment or change are helpful to them, and to you.

Some tasks will require more time than others, for example independent written work or practical activities. Teacher talk, or activities in which students are required to listen are more effective when kept fairly brief.

For a rough guideline, think about splitting your lesson into three sections: time for *listening* (teacher-led discussion, reading activities); time for *exploring* (group activities, discussion, brainstorming, researching, modelling an example); and time for *consolidating* (independent activities, written or practical, sharing information).

Always give clear instructions regarding the amount of time allocated for each activity, enabling students to know what is expected of them. Give adequate warning of time allocation coming to an end, allowing students to conclude their work satisfactorily.

If convenient, use different areas of the classroom for different types of activity. It is common for primary classrooms to have an area for 'carpet time', play areas, practical areas, as well as conventional desks. Practical subject rooms may have formal class seating areas as well as practical worktops and in a drama studio or hall, students can assemble or spread out, as necessary.

Take account of the time required to get settled, organize equipment, pack away or make the transition from activity to activity (especially if movement is required). It is helpful to have a clear routine or strategy for this (see Part 3: 'Routines and Procedures' p. 51).

If students are working on an activity for any significant amount of time, or if a lesson is particularly long, consider allowing a short break (in class), in which they can relax and refresh their brains.

Being flexible

Despite best intentions there are no guarantees that a well-prepared lesson will go according to plan. There are so many factors that can interfere with certainty: the mood of the class, the mood of the teacher, the time of day, the weather, the classroom environment, the type of work, incidents of challenging behaviour, the presence (or absence) of certain individuals ... Being flexible is as important to the effective teacher as is being prepared. It is rather like learning to work the gears of a car: with a bit of experience the driver can sense when the engine is beginning to strain and in need of a gear change. Effective teachers are not only able to sense their students losing concentration (the signs are usually fairly obvious!) – they are able to act on it. They can wrap up a task, switch to something else, or change the focus. In other words, they recognize that there is no point in flogging a dead horse. They combine their own management of the lesson pace and structure with common sense. Although it often relies on momentary intuition, there are ways in which you can *prepare* to be flexible.

- Keep a bank of 'emergency' worksheets, in case your attentions are required elsewhere (for instance, dealing with a severe disruption).
- Anticipate any problems students may have in terms of understanding an idea or task, therefore preparing you to deal with any confusion.
- Have additional tasks or activities in mind for students that complete work quickly.
- Do not be afraid to stop all activity if you feel the class are losing it. It is far more effective to establish a complete hiatus, get everyone's attention, get them to be quiet and calm for five minutes, and then allow them to resume work refocused; than to constantly compete with continuing distraction.
- Use your judgement: tasks that work with some classes may not work with others – assume nothing!
- Use common sense: if the weather is blowing a gale outside, or there has been a big fight at lunchtime, it is very possible that students will be in an excitable mood. Is it wise to attempt that complex and demanding writing activity, or can you substitute it for something more instantly accessible? (Time for those Christmas word searches . . .)
- Learn from mistakes: if certain activities are repeatedly problematic, are they serving a purpose? Likewise, if activities go particularly well, use and develop them.

5 Keeping yourself motivated . . .

Alert and ready – every morning – Monday to Friday. In teaching, it does not do to regularly turn up with a raging hangover, having had two hours' sleep and leftover kebab for breakfast. If you are taking a lesson it is likely that you will want to be on form, not just because the students will suffer otherwise . . . because *you* will. Anyone that has battled with a morning of back-to-back bottom-set 13 year olds, the day after the staff do, will know the pain I speak of! There is nowhere to run and hide, lie low or become incommunicado. In teaching, you are always on show, always performing.

It is not just a party lifestyle that can interfere with the required daily brightness: family commitments, relationship pressures, emotional and physical health issues, an excessive workload or simply feeling a bit jaded – all of these factors can complicate the challenge of staying on top in the classroom. In this chapter, I will look at a selection of ways to successfully manage time and responsibility, and therefore alleviate some of the pressure – but unfortunately this does not include a failproof cure for hangovers!

Planning and preparation

'Planning' used to be a dirty word in my vocabulary. The guidelines given to me during my training consisted of four detailed A4 pages per lesson – it would take me one hour to put together a half-hour session! Much of the information in these epics would just add to my confusion, or never be used. It took several years before I actually started to produce planning that I felt was really useful to me, but when I did, it transformed my teaching.

Good planning should be making life easier for you, not harder. If the time spent doing it outweighs its usefulness, something is amiss! On the other hand, if you feel you are constantly leaping from one unstructured, disorganized lesson to another – perhaps you are not doing enough.

Good planning should be a workable. Include the information that you need, leave out what is superfluous – with practice you'll establish what is useful to you. If necessary, review the format of your planning sheets, and explore ways of making them as user-friendly and accessible as possible.

Good planning should be a working document. There is no point in producing a terms worth of thoughtful, wordprocessed planning sheets that are placed in a file and forgotten about. Keep them to hand. Make notes on them about what has and has not been achieved, who's been absent, who needs to catch up – use them to inform next week's planning.

There are three different levels of planning that can enable you to organize your programme of study: long-, medium- and short-term. Planning in this way provides a solid underlying structure of development and allows you to stagger the workload throughout the year. It also means you coordinate the cycle of topics with the rest of your department or year group, and perhaps even spread the workload between you.

Long-term planning

This is your annual cycle of topics. In consultation with government guidelines, decide what topics and themes need to be covered for each term, taking into account exam preparation and coursework requirements. Having an overall plan for the year, as opposed to doing it as you go along, enables you to establish a clear cycle of progression, and allows you to prepare ahead. If you know what is coming, you can accumulate resources over time, rather than having a last-minute panic.

Medium-term planning

This can be done at the start of every half term/term, and is a more in depth account of the topics outlined in the long-term plan. Medium-term planning can be the outline of a scheme of work, providing brief week-by-week indications of the key objectives and tasks that need to be addressed. Again, this can be done with your department and allows you to prepare in advance for the term ahead of you; and to structure the pace and content of a project. As medium-term planning provides more general information, it can be reused for different groups.

Short-term planning
This is a more detailed breakdown of individual lessons, and can be done on a weekly, or even daily, basis. It should include the lesson objectives, key vocabulary, tasks to be undertaken (including details of text books, page references, discussion topics, types of activity, differentiated tasks) and homework. In other words, it should contain enough information to enable another teacher to pick up what needs to be done. In addition, it could contain information about the responsibilities undertaken by additional staff, required resources, tips for behaviour and any other reminders. Remember: above all else, planning has to be useful for you.

Organizing your workload

Efficient classroom practice does not begin and end with efficient planning. A harmonious relationship with your workload relies on keeping track of many different things. Knowing what bit of paperwork needs to be done and when, knowing where to find the illusive staple gun, remembering to bring in that all-important video. For some, the habit of organization comes easily; for others, it is a constant struggle – but whether you are a ruthless desk tidier, or a hapless muddle, it pays to get yourself organized. Despite the initial effort required, good organization can help you to cut corners further down the line. Find yourself repeating a familiar topic with new students? How fortunate that you saved and filed masters of all those excellent handmade worksheets...

- Keep an eye out for useful resources: topical television programmes, newspaper articles, Internet sites, images and artefacts.
- Keep a small notebook and pen with you at all times: you

never know when the inspiration to plan a new scheme of work will strike!

- Get into the habit of filing the masters of worksheets or useful photocopies. As they accumulate, try to label and organize the files themselves, helping you to find things at a moment's notice.
- If you travel between different classrooms, carry a pack of your own stationery with you, including emergency supplies for forgetful students.
- If handing out stationery or equipment, inform students that you are noting the number of items given out and then count the number given back in − otherwise you may one day open your drawer to find a startling absence of the necessaries.
- Have an unfinished worksheet tray, for incomplete work that students can retrieve and finish at a later date, saving you from having to hunt around.
- Keep your desk space clear and tidy − it's a psychological thing!
- Save time and stress on Monday morning: on Fridays avoid rushing out of the door at the first opportunity and try to prepare your classroom/planning for the following week − the pub will still be there when you are done!
- Streamline your filing: find a system that is simple to administer and get rid of the mess/files/paperwork you never use. That includes clearing out your pigeon hole on a frequent basis.
- Have places to put things, such as files for each important aspect of your classroom practice:
  1. Your current planning file, which should include separate sections for long-term planning, schemes of work, short-term planning, class lists, timetables and homework schedules.
  2. If applicable, your tutor group/pastoral file and your assessment file (containing all the necessary information regarding student attainment and progress: class lists, homework, coursework and exam grades, levels, comments).

3. Your SEN file (IEPs and information about the special needs students you teach).
4. You may also wish to keep files for worksheets or photocopies, and old planning (subject by subject if you are a primary teacher).
5. DO NOT keep a file for miscellaneous items – they are miscellaneous for a reason. Either they have a rightful home or they should be passed on!

Pacing your workload

Time-management is critical in a job where many different things need to be juggled at once and the deadlines are continuous, but it also plays an important role in terms of alleviating pressure – if you are able to pace your workload and use your time wisely, you will avoid those panic-stricken 'I haven't done it' moments. And more importantly, you will feel you have some control over your responsibilities – giving you the strength and stability to battle successfully with the busiest times.

Balance your week
A typical week will have a few easy days, a few busy days, and one ultra nasty day (usually a Monday!). Once you have sussed out the ebb and flow of your timetable, it is possible to organize your workload so that the demands are balanced more evenly. On the toughest teaching days, try to keep other commitments to a minimum. On 'easy' days, take on those other duties/do your chasing up/run a lunchtime club/put in that extra hour...

Balance your day
Plan for your sanity! If you are anticipating a difficult lesson, or a complicated activity, try to plan something straightforward for the classes before and after, allowing you to reserve your energy for where it is needed most.

Use your non-contact time
There will, of course, be times when all you can do is flop down on the most comfortable staffroom chair and chat about

the television you used to watch as a child. Relaxing and enjoying the company of your colleagues is an effective way of recharging your batteries and bringing some 'lite' into a stressful environment – but make sure you know the difference between essential rest and laziness! Although it may be sparse or awkwardly timed, non-contact can always be productive if you want it to be. A half hour here or there can give you the chance to make those phone calls, tidy your files or research an idea. Longer stretches of time can be used for reports, planning or marking – if you are easily distracted, find somewhere quiet.

Plan for your time

It can be helpful to use your regular non-contact time for regular tasks. For example, planning (Thursday, periods 6, 7 and 8) and marking (Monday, periods 3 and 4) as timetabling a routine will give you some comforting structure and enable you to prioritize effectively. If you commit to this effort, you can reward yourself with some guilt-free 'down time' later in the week, knowing that you have earned it.

Little and often, or one big burst

Different approaches work for different people; establish what makes you the most productive you can be. Some people hate the thought of slogging away at paperwork for hours on end: little and often may be the cure. Others would prefer to have one big concentrated effort, and then free themselves up for the rest of the week.

Respect your momentum

There may be times when you feel suddenly inspired: it is well past your home time and you have seen something on the Internet that motivates you to write an entire scheme of work – go with it! For all the nuggets of genius that strike you at 5 pm, there will be stretches of time in which your energy levels are so low you can barely lift a pen, let alone write with it!

'DO IT NOW'

If, like me, you are one of life's procrastinators, use this as your mantra. Every time a little piece of admin comes your way, remind yourself of your mantra and act on it! It is amazing how much time it can take to do things that actually take no time at all.

Never take work home with you
If you want to avoid the feeling that teaching is taking over your life, don't let it. Simple.

Part 3

Routines and Procedures

6 Five essentials . . .

When observing other teachers, I have frequently noticed that the ones struggling the most tend to have a lack of unified procedures and routines. At crucial moments during the lesson or day the organization of the class is left to chance, rather than structure. If I had to suggest one thing that would make classroom life easier for the teacher (and the student), it would be the establishment of certain routines. Routines allow both you and your class to operate in a structured, organized way, helping to remove the confusion and clutter that so often leads to problems.

If students enter a classroom unclear about what is expected of them or how they are to go about it, they will bumble around, seemingly wasting time. If they feel some slack in the reigns, they may well be tempted to indulge in inappropriateness. Setting up routines will counter this problem and create a sense of structure within your class. They will help you to be consistent and focused, enabling your students to understand what is expected of them – and what they can expect from you. Routines will be of particular benefit to students that have emotional and behavioural problems, or difficulties organizing themselves: familiar patterns can reduce anxiety and consolidate boundaries.

If you feel your classroom may be aided by the use of routine, think about when/where it is most needed. Times of transition (changes in activity or location, returning from break, clearing away, getting started, etc.) seem to cause the most stress, but these situations can be easily tamed if you invest some energy into tightening them up. Here are some suggestions for getting to grips with the most delicate classroom moments.

Beginnings

The beginning of a lesson sets the precedent for the rest of its duration, therefore it is important to put some thought into it. I have divided the suggestions for dealing with beginnings into three sections: entering the classroom, getting settled, and addressing 'latecomers'. The important thing to remember is that this is your chance, as the teacher, to assert your role within the classroom. At first, or with a new class, you may find yourself working quite hard; but if you are consistent, your students will learn to recognize what is expected of them.

Entering the classroom

Whether your students line up formally, stand behind their chairs, or come in and sit themselves down, the important thing is that they take their cue from you. Make your expectations utterly clear and stick by them. Quiet. Quick. Sensible. If any individual, or the class in general, fails to achieve this, make them do it again. And again. And again and again, if necessary. Make it clear that you are prepared to pull them in if the standard is not high enough – but do not forget to give acknowledgment and praise when they get it right. Having students line up before entering the room makes the process easier. If they line up, you have the opportunity to establish order and assert your expectations *before* they enter the room. Additionally, you may wish to stagger the flow of students going through the door (girls first/table by table/five at a time).

Getting them settled

So what happens once the students have entered the room? With so much going on – coats to be hung up, pencil cases to be pulled out, seats to be found – things can seem chaotic. Instead of yelling at them to hurry, make some allowance for the time it takes to get organized. The time can be minimized if you issue some simple reminders, for example: 'OK class. As soon as you enter the room you need to take off your coats, get sat down, and take out your planners. Coat. Seat. Planner. Let's see how quickly you can do that . . .' Try setting a time limit (2 to 3 minutes), and encourage students to achieve this, or better it! Once they are properly settled, the opening formalities can begin. Do not address the whole class or start the register before this occurs – expect their full attention otherwise you will lose the momentum. I have seen far too many teachers allow students to casually chat their way through the register call: a chance to rekindle break time interests and distracting gossip ... and throw all the effort taken to get the class in quietly right out of the window! An effective alternative to sitting in silence (for some classes that can be very difficult) is to have them engage with a simple activity as soon as they are at their desks: copying down the date/lesson objectives/homework, or perhaps solving an anagram or word puzzle.

Latecomers

There is always some inane reason why a student has to be late, and they always seem to arrive just as you are getting into your flow. Rather than sidetrack yourself into a lengthy conversation about why the PE teacher had to keep little Robbie behind for 20 minutes (about the time it takes to get to the wasteland behind the mobile classroom and smoke a cigarette), have the student wait at the door, until you are free to talk to them; or request that they sit down and get started with an ominous 'We'll talk about the reason for your lateness after class!' Avoid allowing students to drift into the classroom as they please. The late arrival of certain characters can sometimes upset the balance, if an individual rouses interest because they have been in trouble, or chooses to strike up conversation as they saunter between the desks. Vigilance will prevent this from getting out of hand.

Endings

Finishing your lesson in a structured way is equally important, as it reinforces your ability to maintain control and minimizes the risk of behavioural problems – at a time when students are likely to be tired and restless, and therefore more prone to mishap. Of course, there will be lessons where you lose track of time (owing to the wonderfully enthusiastic learning that has been taking place!), resulting in a hurried mass exit. But if most of your endeavours lead to a clean, organized conclusion, then you students will get the general idea.

Prepare for the end!
Always account for the time it takes to pack away. Experience will help you to judge how long it may take in any given circumstances, but remember that clearing up complex practical tasks could take 10 minutes or so. Ensure that your students are prepared for the end as well. Alert them to the amount of time they have left to complete an activity, or even provide a visual reference such as an egg timer or stopwatch. Remember to be flexible: if students are particularly absorbed by a task – use your judgement – you may decide that the benefits of their enthusiasm outweigh an efficient clear up.

Recap
Ideally, the last few minutes of a lesson should see the students sat at their tidy desks, calm and ready to be dismissed. The timing can be tricky: misjudge it and you may find you have your students staring blankly back at you for five minutes or more – which can seem like a long time, once your teaching energy has been spent! It is, however, a golden opportunity to recap on what has been learned during the lesson, to remind students of homework (although I would recommend setting the homework at the start of the lesson) or commenting on behaviour – expressing praise or 'hope' for improvement (make it positive).

Dismiss with care
Many effective teachers keep tight control right to the end, ensuring that their students leave the classroom as calmly as they were made to enter it. Avoid a mass bundle for the door by dismissing students table by table, row, or even individual, at a time. If you are feeling playful, make a game of it: 'Students with the letter "P" in their name can go first/students wearing blue socks/students who got 8 out of 10 or more in the test ...' In the primary classroom, children should learn good habits, lining up at the door, whenever entering or exiting the classroom.

Moving about the classroom

Managing the movement of students around the classroom can save a lot of time, and spare some of your patience. The risk of problematic behaviour occurring always increases at unstructured points of the day/lesson, such as the moments in which students are in 'transition' – if you can organize these moments in a structured way, you will prevent some of the problems from manifesting. It is particularly important in the younger primary classroom, where students may be moving from their desks to the book corner/carpet area/art table on a frequent basis. Although secondary lessons are often more static, certain subjects and certain activities call for considerable amounts of transition – it is helpful to have a sense of control over this. Here are some suggestions for organizing movement, which can be applied in a variety of circumstances:

Wait for the cue

Remind students that they are to move when you ask them to – there will always be a few that jump up eagerly. Give them the necessary instructions, check that they understand – *pause* – and then ask them to get underway. A pause allows you to establish a sense of calm before proceeding.

Stagger the dismissal

If students are required to move from one area of the classroom to another, instruct them to do so table by table – avoiding a chaotic rush. This gives you greater opportunity to monitor their behaviour, and maintain a sense of order.

Keep watch

Make students feel that they are under observation, even though there may be lots of distractions in the room: 'I'm watching to see how sensibly you can get sat at your desks.' Emphasize your expectations regarding how they move around.

Use your efficient students

While taking the register or introducing the lesson, send a few reliable, or for an alternative approach, difficult students to set out equipment (e.g., art materials, calculators, text books) in advance of the rest of the group starting the activity. This minimizes the need for large groups of students to be trying to collect equipment at once.

Set specific time limits
Instruct students that they have one/two/five minutes to get themselves organized and ready to begin. Turn it into a challenge – who can be ready fastest?

Emphasise health and safety
Reiterate to students how important it is to move carefully and sensibly around the classroom. This is particularly important during practical activities.

Minimize unnecessary movement
Encourage students to remain seated and raise their hand if they need assistance. There is nothing more frustrating than a gaggle of children following you round the classroom, and whingeing – learning to be patient is lesson worth learning.

Getting attention

If attention is the currency of the classroom, make sure you are the banker! By establishing clear protocols for how you give it and how you get it, you can ensure that your students do not take advantage of you. I have divided this section into two parts, initially focusing on ways in which the teacher can gain student attention; followed by suggestions for encouraging students to request teacher attention in appropriate ways.

Here are some ways of gaining student attention.

Wait for silence
Really, this should stand to reason, but it is painfully common to see teachers trying to stretch a list of instructions over the top of a semi-quiet rabble. Do not do it! If you are addressing the class, expect their full attention. Take them to task if they are struggling, but never start a lesson without the minimum courtesy of every single one of your students at least looking

like they are listening. Indeed, it can be one of the hardest things to achieve, but it is an essential part of your classroom control. Doing it properly (even if it takes up considerable time) will send out a clear message about your expectations, and will save time and energy in the long run.

Use cues

There are many ways you can show you want full student attention which provide alternatives to raising your voice. If used consistently, students will recognize these cues and respond accordingly.

1. Count down from ten or five, using your voice and/or your fingers.
2. Raise your hand up, and hold it until students take notice.
3. Finger on lips, students have to copy the action as soon as they notice. Eventually the entire class should follow suit.
4. The 'look'. Stand ominously at the front of the class, and just work that facial expression!
5. Look bored. Fold your arms, look at your watch, mutter to yourself about how disappointing it is that time is being wasted ... perhaps it can be made up after school?
6. Set up a routine. For example, students need to be quiet and listening by the time you have finished writing 'Thank you for paying attention!' on the whiteboard.
7. With younger students, try singing a song (!) that they have to join in with – thereby cajoling everyone into focusing on you. 'Head, Shoulders, Knees and Toes' or the like ...
8. Use a loud sound, such as a bell or alarm (a hotel reception bell works very well), to signal that you want student attention.

Emphasize listening skills

Some students will benefit from reminders about how to focus their attention – it does not come naturally to everyone. Ask them to 'show' you that they are listening by looking at you, making eye contact, putting equipment or stationery down and sitting up straight. This is relevant to communicating with individual students as well as with groups.

Have activities ready

Some classes can be very difficult to settle and focus at the start of a session. If getting them to listen to you straight away is proving difficult, try setting out a simple 'calming' activity (e.g., a key vocabulary word search, crossword or maths puzzle) that is there, on the desk, waiting for them as they enter the room – something that needs no explanation from you, but will suitably absorb their attention and draw them into a more focused mind set. Once they are better settled, you can introduce the main lesson.

Be firm and follow up

Some teachers will complain that they have tried everything to get their students to pay attention to them – but nothing seems to have a long-lasting effect. The fact is none of the methods suggested above will make a significant difference unless your students respect you. They will only respect you if you are firm, consistent and true to your word. Once you have established your routines and expectations with the class, be rigorous in sticking to them.

Here are some ways for the students to gain the teacher's attention.

Encourage good manners

Minimize disruption by encouraging students to raise their hand and wait if they wish to speak to an adult (unless it is an emergency). Alternatively, ask them to come out and speak to you at your desk; but avoid having students wandering around the room as they try to chase up your attention. It will be irritating to you and risks the distraction of other students – hence the phrase 'Why are you out of your chair?' chimes from classrooms up and down the country . . .

Encourage independence

With the considerable demands placed on your time and energy, it is always worth encouraging students to take responsibility for themselves. Do they really need you to help them decide what colours to do their bubble writing in, or can they seek the advice of a friend?

Adopt systems

Avoid unnecessary questions and concerns by setting up routine systems for organizing student workload. Have specific trays where completed work can be placed, ready for marking; and have a tray of extension worksheets or follow-up activities that will service the quick workers – saving you from fishing around for bits of paper, and answering the same question ('what shall I do now?') 15 times!

Reinforce positive attention

Give students attention for the right reasons; withdraw it for the wrong ones. In other words, encourage good behaviour by acknowledging and responding to it. Show disinterest in less positive bids for your attention; redirect them towards ways in which they *could* impress you.

Solving conflict

Having a structured way of dealing with arguments and difficulties is beneficial to both you and your students. For you, it provides a framework, which may reduce the amount of confusion and stress that such situations can create – knowing that you can tackle a problem in a systematic tried-and-tested way will help you to remain calm and in control. For your students, a routine may represent security and fairness, which will give them confidence in you and your willingness to bring about justice. Here are some suggestions for setting up a protocol of tackling disputes and difficulties.

Discuss the problem

If students are arguing or winding each other up, do not assume you know what has happened and who is at fault. Establish calm and then talk it through. If necessary, request that they discuss the matter with you at your desk, or outside the door (neutral territory, away from other interfering students).

Let them have their say

Give each individual involved in the argument/incident a chance to put forward their version of events – even if they produce a bunch of incorrigible lies, there are lessons to be learned. Make sure that everyone in the discussion gets an uninterrupted turn (good practice for listening skills), and conclude with your over-arching wisdom on the matter, eliciting a consensus about who has done what and why.

Focus on moving forward

Once you have established what has happened, encourage students to reflect on the problem and seek resolution. Focus on three key questions.

1. What has happened?
2. How can I put it right?
3. What will I do if it happens again?

Some students will benefit from consolidating these thoughts in written form. Consider preparing a conflict resolution sheet that students have to fill in and then share with you. Be mindful of the fact that students with low literacy may struggle with this.

Expect apology

Encourage students to make amends through apology, whether it is to you or to one another. Although it is only a symbolic gesture, a sincere apology can be a powerful way of getting a student to take responsibility for their actions. Apologies can be verbal, but for more serious problems, written ones may be appropriate.

7 Establishing boundaries...

One of the key pieces of armour in the battle against inappropriate behaviour is the establishment of clear boundaries: what is acceptable, what is not. Boundaries are established through common understanding between those setting them and those following them. In order to bring about this understanding, it is important to be consistent and clear about what you want from your students. Do not assume that they will automatically know – many students are well aware of acceptable codes of behaviour, but others may not have the same level of insight. If a child has grown up in an environment that lacks sufficient boundaries, they may struggle to identify them in the classroom.

Your own sense of your boundaries needs to be strong, for there will be certain individuals who feel urged to test them on a regular basis. Underpin them with some organized thinking, and they will be easier to define; in other words, know what *you* want. Most importantly, the existence of boundaries needs to translate to the student consciousness – a systematic approach will help you to promote them. Here are some suggestions for helping you to establish, apply and maintain effective boundaries.

Class rules, rights and responsibilities

For many people, the starting point for managing behaviour and establishing boundaries is setting a list of rules. In addition to rules, contemporary thinking incorporates the more holistic concepts of 'rights' and 'responsibilities'. Whatever form they take, however, they are next to useless if they are not workable or made use of. I grit my teeth whenever I see a struggling teacher claim they have class rules, only to find that these rules consist of a tatty sheet of typed A4, pinned to the back of the door. If rules are not active or accessible, why bother making them? Rules, rights and responsibilities can exist at different levels and serve different purposes. Here are some suggestions.

Rules, rights and responsibilities for the whole school

The document in question is the school behaviour policy. This policy should function as a set of guidelines for encouraging positive behaviour around the school. Every school should have one, though they can vary in quality and approach. A helpful behaviour policy should be a working document, one that is regularly revisited and reviewed. It should also be something that everyone has a sense of ownership over; therefore rules are brought about through agreement rather than dictation. During the development of the policy, everyone involved with its use should be consulted regarding its content: management, governors, teachers, assistants, ancillary staff, parents and students. Make sure you are familiar with your school rules – I have encountered a worryingly large number of teachers who have never even seen a copy of their school's behaviour policy!

Rules, rights, and responsibilities for class

Class rules need the same consideration and attention as whole-school rules, although they operate within the smaller, specific environment of the classroom. A useful starting point for establishing a classroom code of behaviour is to look at the 'rights' of the individuals within the class (including staff!). For example:

1. Everyone in this classroom has the right to learn.
2. Everyone in this classroom has the right to feel respected.
3. Everyone in this classroom has the right to feel safe.

Once the rights have been decided upon, it is possible to relate them to certain 'responsibilities'. For example, members of the class have:

1. The responsibility to let the teacher teach.
2. The responsibility to listen and learn, and allow others to do the same.
3. The responsibility to be helpful to others.
4. The responsibility to be kind to others.
5. The responsibility to look after the classroom.
6. The responsibility to solve problems in a sensible way.

From the important responsibilities it is possible to develop a correlating set of 'rules' that will help students to follow their duty. For example:

1. Always move sensibly around the classroom.
2. Remember to raise your hand instead of interrupting the teacher.
3. Tidy equipment away when you have finished with it.
4. If you are having a difficulty, ask an adult for help.

These rules should be phrased positively where possible, and should always be relevant to what is happening in the classroom. Certain key issues may be covered by the whole-school policy (such as uniform, moving around the corridors, break time behaviour, lateness), which you can refer to as necessary – they will not need to be restated in the class rules. Keep it simple and workable.

Rules for certain things
Certain environments will call for specific organization of behaviour. Drama halls, PE changing rooms, science labs and workshops, to name a few, will need special consideration when it comes to rules. In addition to the general code of behaviour, rules relating to health and safety, use of equipment or access to different areas, will need to be applied.

Repetition

In this section I will focus on how to make use of the rules, rights and responsibilities. It is easy to produce a well thought out list; the hard part is making this list meaningful – but without being meaningful, it might as well not exist. If rules are to be active, they will need to be a regular feature in your classroom practice. Repeat. Revisit. Review. It is not particularly complicated; it just requires time (which, unfortunately, is always at a premium in the classroom). When working in a SEN school with very challenging students, my colleagues and I have occasionally taken the measure of temporarily cutting out some of the curriculum, in order to focus on developing appropriate classroom conduct and establishing boundaries. Without receiving intense attention to this aspect of their schooling, these students would have had significantly limited access to the curriculum anyway – too busy lobbing chairs at each other! Although this is an extreme situation, it hopefully highlights the value of making behaviour management an integral part of your teaching career.

Repeat

The most effective way to ensure that the class rules and boundaries are implanted in the student consciousness is to keep them circulating. Refer to them frequently and consistently.

1. Once they have been established they can be highlighted when dealing with individual or class behaviour. Either a simple reminder: 'Class, please remember our rule for walking sensibly around the classroom!' or a clarification: 'Andrew, I'm not happy that you have ignored our rule about speaking politely to one another. You need to remind yourself why it is important … remember, everyone in this classroom has a right to be respected. By calling people names, you are spoiling that right for someone else. How would you feel if someone was being disrespectful to you?'

2. Rules should also be referred to positively: 'Well done! Everyone has paid attention to our rule about being quiet today, which has really helped us to get on with our work.'

3. Remember, rules are most effective when they are applied consistently. For example, if a school chooses to promote a strict uniform code and every member of staff upholds it, students will be less able to flaunt their

'alternative' clothes. If staff are inconsistent in maintaining this rule, conflict and confusion will almost certainly arise.

Revisit

Many teachers will spend time discussing class rules and expectations during initial meetings with a new class. It is helpful to revisit this experience at the start of each term, or whenever you sense that the rulebook needs refreshing. To ensure that the discussion has the necessary impact, it may be helpful to make more of the occasion than simply giving a monologue. Here are some suggestions.

1. For older children, begin with a brainstorming session about 'rights'. What are they? Why are they important? Establish some 'rights' for members of the class. This can lead to further discussion: how can we make sure that people have their rights respected? By being 'responsible' of course. Ask students to suggest what their responsibilities should be. What would help us to carry out these responsibilities? Having some reminders/rules about how to behave ... By going through this process, you will be encouraging your students to understand *why* we need to follow rules.

2. Younger children may benefit from visual reminders. Having decided on helpful class rules, spend a lesson or two putting together a display. Depending on the age group, this can be bright and fluffy or eye-catching and cool: smiley faces and visual images – as long as the information is clear. Another idea would be to photograph students enacting certain dos and don'ts, providing a fun visual resource, and also using role-play to get them engaging with the process.

3. A more formal approach would be to agree on the rights and rules, and then them have typed into 'contracts' for each class member to sign. This emphasizes a collaborative approach to rule making and maintenance, but in itself is not enough for certain individuals who may struggle to comprehend the 'binding' effect of putting a signature on a piece of paper!

Review

If the rules are not getting through in the way that they should, it may be worth reviewing their appropriateness and changing or developing them as necessary. Do they need simplifying? Are they tackling the real cause of disruption? Do they cover everything? Has the behaviour and attitude of the class changed thereby certain rules are no longer relevant? Does a change of environment or activity require additional attention? Remember, they need to be 'workable' in order to be effective. A system of rules does not have to be static, but any changes you make should be clearly communicated to your students ... otherwise confusion will ensue.

Reward systems

In addition to clearly defined boundaries, another routine practice that will aid behaviour management is the rewarding of positive action. No prizes for guessing that a reward system needs to be consistent, fair and workable if it is to be effective. It can exist in different forms and be applied in different ways (points charts, certificates, stickers, prizes), as long as its existence and application is transparent and clear to the individuals it affects. I have seen several different reward systems operated at once: points out of five for each table per lesson, extra 'choosing time' for students that listen well, special certificates for good attendance, small prize for the best student at the end of the week (at the teachers' discretion) and overall class points working towards a trip at the end of the month ... While no one could dispute this teacher's willingness to offer incentives, having so many different systems will make the process more complicated and confusing than it needs to be – for both the teacher and the students. Keep it simple. Establish a structured system that is easy to apply, and will cover different aspects of class activity. Many effective systems involve students accumulating points/merits over time, leading to a specific reward or prize. When setting up such a system, ask yourself these questions:

1. Who are you rewarding?
2. What are you rewarding them for?
3. When are you rewarding them?
4. How are you rewarding them?

Let's look at the first of these questions: who are you rewarding?

Whole school

Increasingly, schools are beginning to recognize the value of rewarding students, and are establishing whole-school systems, such as 'merit awards'. Students accumulate merits from teachers (often noted in the student's planner, with the teachers initials or a special stamp), and will receive acknowledgement and reward as their collection increases; for example, 20 merits equals a certificate, 50 merits equals a mention in assembly, 100 merits equals tea with the Head (now that's an opportunity most staff members don't get!). Some schools offer savvy prizes: stationary, shopping vouchers, even mountain bikes! The benefits of a whole-school system are that it encourages consistent practice among staff, creates a unified school ethos and does a lot of the work for you; all you need to do is remember to give out the merits as necessary. It can, however, be slightly impersonal and may alienate students with low self-esteem, who will automatically (and perhaps realistically) assume that the possibility of the shiny mountain bike belongs to everyone else but them.

Whole class

A reward system specific to you and your students can strengthen the classroom relationship and reinforce your expectations. In a class of 20 to 30, it is unreasonable to imagine that you could provide an individual points breakdown for each student every lesson – reward points/merits to each table (if they sit in the same places every lesson) or the class as a whole. Rewarding students in this way can encourage teamwork and group cohesion, but be aware that it can also create tension, if a few individuals consistently let the group down.

Individuals

A system that awards points/merits to each individual student provides a very personalized, attentive approach to reward; and will enable you to address the motivations and needs of every child. This is particularly important when working with students with SEN. Although an individualized approach can be impractical for large classes, it is ideal for small group settings, such as LSUs. If you have challenging students in your mainstream class, it is possible to set up personalized reward systems specific to these individuals (as long as the rest of the class understand the reason for this singularity and receive adequate whole-class rewards themselves), enabling you to monitor and address individual need.

An alternative would be to have individual star/sticker charts for every student, therefore including everyone. Each time a student does something noteworthy give them a sticker to add to their chart; when the chart is complete they are given a reward. This system is the most inclusive, while allowing students to develop at their own pace and for you to address individual achievements. For secondary teachers, it is somewhat impractical (how many individual sticker charts?) and may not appeal to the streetwise older youth ... although you may be surprised (I have watched many a 13-year-old squeal with delight as they receive their 'I'm an ace reader' stickers!).

Now let's address the second question: what are you rewarding them for?

General activity

Although it is not feasible to pass a judgement of merit over every single event that occurs during a lesson, it is always worth having a few distinctions: work and behaviour, effort and achievement. For example, for a potential total of ten points per lesson, five could be associated with class behaviour, and five can be awarded for actual work. If this is done consistently, students will recognize where there opportunities for success lie. It allows you to be flexible, and importantly, enables you to clarify what your students are doing right.

Specific situations

Certain events during the school day may require additional attention. In the ESBD class, lining up after break was always fraught with problems; therefore it was agreed that in addition to lesson points, the class would receive 'lining up' points. If your students have problems with specific situations, consider whipping them into shape with the incentives of a point/reward system: assembly, pastoral periods, lining up, break times (though difficult to monitor), movement around the school/class, tidying up, entering the room or PE changing rooms.

Particular contributions

When operating a reward system that addresses the progress of the whole class, it is still possible to acknowledge individual heroics. For example: 'This lesson, some of you were a little bit rowdy when you came in and it took longer than usual for everyone to settle – but you were quiet and cooperative for the rest of the time, so I will give you four out of five for your behaviour. However, it has come to my attention that Naseem was particularly helpful to another student that was having difficulty understanding the work today ... because of his kind contribution, I am going to award an extra point. So that's a total of five – well done class! And special thanks to Naseem for making that possible ...'

Individual progress and achievement

In a class of students with mixed ability and need, it is important to make allowances for personal achievements. Some students will be making very small improvements, whilst others will be leaping ahead – avoid comparisons and focus on individual progress. It is also important to acknowledge effort, even if the ultimate result is unsatisfactory. This counts for aspects of behaviour as well as work: during a difficulty, if a student at least *tries* to do the right thing, draw positive attention to it.

Now let's consider the third question when setting up an incentive scheme: when are you rewarding them?

Every lesson

Consistently factoring in time to discuss and record class/merit points at the end of every session, will maintain the relevance of the process. Regular calculation and reminders will keep the incentive going. Think about how progress will be recorded. It may be helpful to have a points record that can be filled in on a daily/weekly basis. For younger students a chart or bar graph on the wall may provide that all-important visual encouragement.

Regular and small

For more challenging students, it can be helpful to have a system that provides frequent incentives to earn points. For example, my own class were able to earn 'bonus time' at the end of each morning: up to ten minutes of time spent on a chosen activity (such as games, computers, drawing), assuming all other work was completed and behaviour had merited such opportunity (they would earn points for work and behaviour, each point equalling one minute of bonus time). This system came about after several months of experimentation, and proved to be extremely effective. The fact that the reward came daily, immediately after the mornings' work, made it attainable and tangible; helping these students, with otherwise poor concentration spans, to retain motivation and focus.

The long haul

For more able students, or for a special purpose, your reward system may head towards one large prize at the end of an extended period of effort: an end-of-term party, trips or special assemblies. This is an effective way of getting students to be self-disciplined, and to think about the long-term consequences of their actions. However, it can prove problematic for some individuals. If a student struggles with self-control, they may find it difficult to sustain good behaviour and could easily lose sight of the ultimate reward, fearing they will never reach it.

And finally: how are you rewarding them?

Systematically

Whether you are issuing points, stickers, stars or merits, etc., it is vital that you establish how students are to accrue them. If, for example, you are using a points system, you will need to clarify a few things:

1. Will there be a maximum amount that students can earn per lesson/day/week, or will points continue to build throughout the week/term/year?
2. How many will they need in order to receive a special prize/incentive?
3. Will they be able to earn bonus points, if they reach the maximum?
4. Will all students automatically start with maximum points (a positive beginning) which can be lost? Or will they all start with nothing and have to earn them?
5. If they lose points, can they earn them back again? They will inevitably ask this question – so think carefully, be firm, and whatever you decide, stick with it.
6. Once earned, can they be taken away?

Clearly
Whenever you are rewarding a student, be very clear about what you are rewarding them for – associate the positive behaviour with positive attention. Likewise, if a student has had difficulties and, thereby, missed out on rewards, be specific about why this has happened.

With incentive
Choose incentives that you consider to be appropriate, practical and appealing to your students. Some may favour 'stuff' (small prizes: stickers, chocolate bars, key rings, etc.), others may do better working towards 'time'. Other incentives could be trips, favoured activities, acknowledgment through certificates or a mention in assembly. Be prepared to overhaul you reward and incentive system if necessary – students can have a habit of losing interest over time.

Verbally
The most important reward you can give – one that should be provided regardless of any other systems you have set up – is praise, good old-fashioned praise!

Sanctions

The use of sanctions to address difficult behaviour can be quite contentious. Personally, I believe they have a useful function as long as they are used judiciously and seen as a way of encouraging students to make better choices and make amends, rather than 'punishment'. They should be viewed as the consequences of a child's actions. Here are some suggestions for making sanctions/consequences helpful to your classroom management practice.

Make them appropriate

Ensure that the intensity of the consequence reflects the seriousness of the 'crime'. It may help to establish some stock consequences, therefore making it easier for you to be fair and consistent. Sometimes it is necessary to give them a bit of a shock (if the behaviour has been particularly inappropriate):

1. Loss of points/merits.
2. Send them to the deputy head/head.
3. A phone call home.
4. Asking them to write a letter of apology.
5. Withdrawal of privileges (e.g., a trip, certain activities).

Sometimes it is a matter of wasting their time (to make up for the waste of yours):

1. After-school detention (in silence).
2. Litter picking at lunchtime.
3. Staying behind at break to complete unfinished work/ write lines.
4. Tidying the classroom (although some students will enjoy this!).

See them through

Whatever consequences you set, you need to make sure they are enacted. Issuing a sanction and then forgetting/not bothering to pursue it will undermine your authority like nothing else! If you decide that a student has behaved so well that they have relinquished the sanction imposed on them, fair enough – but make sure this is made explicit to the student, otherwise they may assume they simply 'got away with it'. And do not be fooled by those who go out of their way to be helpful and lovely after you have set them detention. Unless the circumstances are exceptional, I endeavour to operate a 'too late' policy: 'Yes. I appreciate the "you're the nicest teacher in the world" card, but I just don't accept bribes! You do the crime/you do the time ...'

Do not threaten what you cannot deliver

If the idea is to see consequences through, think carefully before you administer them. Remember, it be will you who has to chase the issue up – you may have to give up your break, or use valuable after-school time; which is perfectly convenient on occasion, but if you are prone to outbursts of: 'Right. That's it. You lot are in detention with me every night this week ... I'm not having it anymore!' you may need to learn to bite your tongue.

The sliding scale of intervention

'Sarah. I've had enough of you – GET OUT!'

All too often, I have observed teachers jumping in with both feet and using this kind of terse reaction to misbehaviour. This sort of intervention stems from impatience, frustration and the struggle for power. While I understand the pressure and stress that teachers can be feeling (which can trigger reactions of this kind), it is important to seek ways to tackle behaviour that imply composure, confidence and self-control. You want your students to see that you are unphased by their antics and able to command the situation. Because of this, it is helpful to think of your behaviour management practice as a 'sliding scale' – enabling you to feel in control and for your students to make choices.

Sanctions/consequences should be seen as a last resort when dealing with general difficult behaviour – it is helpful to hold on to your bargaining power. A student should first have the chance to put things right and make amends. If they fail to do this, then they can be sanctioned accordingly, and shown the consequences of their unfortunate behaviour. But without the steps inbetween, they will never learn to take responsibility for themselves and to make good choices.

The two most valuable ways of encouraging students to take responsibility for their actions and regain personal control are withdrawal ('time out') and apology. Although some individuals may show resistance to both of these things, they are not necessarily sanctions and should be viewed positively: a chance to reflect, to regain composure, to calm down, to accept responsibility and to change their attitude *before* treading down the path of disaster! If they fail to do these things adequately or choose to continue with the problematic behaviour, they are making their own unhelpful choice ... let 'em have it.

Here is a guideline to the sliding scale of intervention, assuming you have noticed a student exhibiting some disruptive off-task behaviour. It provides the opportunity for you to use the minimum intervention necessary – which is less stressful and disruptive for you and the class. The important thing is to intervene early – be vigilant and tackle problems before they start developing. If a student responds appropriately to your intervention at any point, the work is hopefully done. If they fail to respond, then move to the next level.

1. *The Look*. Glare at the problem, and make students aware that you are aware of them!
2. *Physical presence*. Move towards the problem, and hover ominously.
3. *Verbal warning*. Quietly tell the student what they need to do/stop doing.
4. *Repeat verbal warning*. Repeat the warning, and explain that if they choose to continue they will have to take some 'time out'.
5. *Time out*. Student to move temporarily to another part of the classroom/outside the door; where they can sit quietly, without disturbance and calm down/reflect. Time out should be no more than five minutes. It is not a punishment; it is a chance to show they are able to comply with classroom conduct. At the end of 'time out',

speak to the student about their behaviour (seek an apology or a demonstration of willingness to make a better effort) and allow them to return to class.

6. *Warning of consequence.* If the student fails to cope with time out, or their behaviour does not improve after taking it, warn them that this will lead to a consequence (detention/loss of points/move to another table/etc.).

7. *Enact consequence.* Set the sanction. Be aware, however, that this may cause further resentment from the student, and will not necessarily make things easier. A way around this would be to request that the student speak to you after class, that you will set the consequence then – suggest that you might take into account their behaviour for the rest of the lesson; if they buck up their ideas they may get a more lenient sentence!

8. *The final straw.* If behaviour continues to deteriorate and the student, despite several chances, is failing to comply with classroom boundaries, it may be necessary to with-draw the student from the lesson entirely – they are not in a frame of mind to learn, and will only disturb others. All schools should have a system for removing students from class, whether they are sent to an office, into another class or to a behaviour support room. After this sanction has been applied, it is important to follow up the process and establish a way for you and the student to move forward.

Part 4

The Classroom Environment

8 Organized chaos or chaotic organization . . .

Whenever I am asked to observe a class, the first thing I am aware of is the state of the room. Often there is enough information here for me to know what kind of experience I am in for. But it is not just me that makes this sort of snap judgement; the appearance and organization of the classroom makes a significant impression on the students too. If a room is bright and welcoming, it will be more appealing. If it is organized and tidy, an expectation about order and respect is being set. If a room is chaotic and/or dreary, it will have a dispiriting effect on the learning process.

The appearance of your classroom can affect the atmosphere of your lessons. Do what works for you and suits your style, but look to provide organization and inspiration. If you are muddling about in a messy, uncared for space – get it sorted. Make an event of it, and have your students help you – create a space that they can be proud of and have some ownership over. This will encourage them to look after it, and may influence their overall behaviour. It will certainly give you something less stressful to look at each morning! I will now consider the benefits of different classroom attributes and how they can be achieved.

The tidy room

Tidiness breeds organization – it is as simple as that. In a messy room, things are easily lost and it can be difficult to keep track of everything that is going on. If you are having to train your eyes to look between piles of scrap paper, unwashed art materials, dead plants and random textbooks, you are making the task of spotting the student that is in the wrong place at the wrong time much harder for yourself.

A tidy, uncluttered space will be an easier space in which to manage your students, and in turn will reduce stress. Moreover, a tidy room can encourage students to respect the environment around them and make an effort to maintain it. If it seems that you have taken pride in the room and made a welcoming space, the majority of your students will follow. Here are some tips for keeping tidy.

- Kick start the process by getting everyone to help out – no, it is not a particularly academic pursuit, but it will help students to develop a sense of pride and ownership over their learning space.
- Clear out old stuff. Be ruthless. Get rid of anything that will not be useful. If you are really not sure about certain items or paperwork, try to find some cupboard space and store it away – if it does not get used during the year, then its uselessness is confirmed: chuck it out.
- Create spaces for different activities: art alley, reading retreat, science street, coat-hook corner, punishment prison? (Mmm . . . perhaps not.)
- Organize/reorganize files for your paperwork, and put them in an accessible place (see 'Organizing your work-load' p. 43).
- Organize classroom stationery into trays, draws or desk tidies; encourage students to put things back appropriately.
- Collect up all stray stationery and get someone to test the pens, felts, etc., and chuck out the broken stuff.
- Laminate posters and signs: preserving their lifespan.
- Label up drawers, cupboards and other storage spaces.
- Run a poster competition for keeping the room tidy (encouraging students to get enthusiastic about being neat).
- Promote clear rules about tidying up.
- Make use of helpers/classroom monitors (many students seem to relish the chance to do 'jobs' for teachers!).
- Incorporate time to tidy up into your lesson planning, ensuring it gets done adequately.

The inspirational room

The inspirational room can be invigorating for your students. If interesting visual stimuli are surrounding them, their curiosity will be fed. Eye-catching displays and helpful information will nurture their interests and encourage independent learning. If they see their own work thoughtfully displayed on the walls, they will feel motivated and proud. A plain room, by contrast, can feel drab, uninviting and impersonal. It misses a valuable opportunity to generate interest and enthusiasm about a topic or subject. Make your room exciting and you will enjoy teaching in it; but be careful, if too much is happening on the walls, it can sometimes be distracting for students. Ah well – better that they are distracted by their imaginations, than by each other! Here are some tips for being inspirational.

- Put up posters from art galleries or museums.
- Organize themed display boards (relevant to whatever topics are being covered). Make these as bold and exciting as you can – a little creative flair can transform the atmosphere of a room.
- If relevant, have a pastoral display area/teachers notice-board reflecting the individuals in your class/tutor group (you could include photographs, birthday lists, etc.).
- Have a class rules and expectations display.
- Mount and display students' work. Change the displays fairly frequently, allowing different individuals to have their moment.
- Temporarily theme the room (e.g., for a history project on ancient Egypt have it decked out as a makeshift temple). Although this requires effort, it is likely to be fun and rewarding.
- Create display areas for models – if decorating the whole room to look like a medieval fortress is too much work, get students to make a class model (e.g., a reconstruction of the Great Fire of London, using just toilet rolls and tissue paper!).
- Keep the area that students generally face (where you stand) simple and unadorned, therefore they can focus their attention on you.

The functional room

Classrooms are busy places, often with several different activities going on at once. They also tend to be storage facilities for all manner of things: some of them vital (such as current resources), some of them occasionally useful (15-year-old textbooks) and some of them just a necessary inconvenience (anything belonging to the students: coats, bags, hairbrushes ...). Having places where necessary resources can be safely stored and easily retrieved is extremely helpful. Being able to move around the room, without tripping over a giant sports bag is also helpful – make your room a convenient, comfortable place to teach in.

- Rearrange the room to suit you. If you take one look at your new classroom and feel deflated by its untidy, awkward design (inherited from your predecessors), look at what you can do to make it a space that you can easily work in. Very feng shui!
- Explore different student seating arrangements. Rows or groups? (Although for some, the arrangement will be dictated by the size/shape of the classroom.) Rows are more formal, and can lead to less distraction, while clusters will facilitate better group activity. Other options include the horseshoe, the big V, or semicircles. Perhaps the best way to make seating arrangements work for you is to avoid rigidity; change the classroom throughout the year, or according to the nature of certain tasks ... keep students on their toes!
- Be flexible. If your room is suitably adaptable, consider how you can regularly vary the arrangement of furniture to facilitate different activities. Enlist the help of students to set up/put back the furniture in the course of the lesson/afternoon, though you need to check that your school policy allows for students to do this.
- In primary classrooms (where many different subjects can be taught in the same space), develop different areas of the classroom for different kinds of activity: creative work (potentially quite messy), computer stations, quiet work, the reading corner, the play area, the science table, etc.

Different areas could even be demarcated with signs or colour codes.

- Ensure there is adequate space for you and your students to walk between desks without having to unduly disturb others. If there is no alternative storage, encourage students to store their bags/coats *safely* under their tables.
- If you require students to line up before leaving the class, ensure that there is a space for them to do this – make sure the space is away from equipment or displays that could be fiddled with while waiting to be dismissed.
- Make sure that students can face you and the board comfortably. Hopefully, the board will be in a position from where you can see everything that is going on.
- Organize personal drawer/cupboard space for students to store their work. Have different folders for finished/ unfinished work. If exercise books are used, have an established place for storing them after each lesson, minimizing the risk of any going 'walkabout'.
- If students bring in personal items (mobile phones, etc.) consider setting up a safety deposit box where valuable (and potentially distracting) items can be placed and stored throughout the lesson/day. This approach has worked very well for me in the past: an effective compromise between the outright ban of phones and the risk of students messing around with them at inappropriate times (although it may be difficult to organize for large groups of students).
- Save time organizing equipment by having essential stationery permanently on tables (in pots or a tray). Place necessary text/exercise books on the tables before the lesson begins (this is easier if you have assistance), therefore saving time when students are about to start working.

Physical comfort

We have all taught, or been taught, in rooms that are too hot and stuffy, too cold, too noisy, too small or too lofty and big. Although school buildings are improving all the time, there are still plenty out there that would benefit from more than just a lick of paint. Unfortunately, some of the problems may be inescapable: how can you get cool air circulating around a room which has windows that are designed to open no more than an inch? And if you are really unfortunate, the same room that sweats like a greenhouse inferno in summer will be chilly as a freezer in winter! The climate of a room can have a significant impact on the energy and concentration levels of those that spend time in it, so it is important to make it as comfortable as possible.

If your room is problematic in this way, do not suffer in silence: make a fuss. No it may not get you anywhere, but then again the kindly caretaker might just find a way of loosening the window screws that have held them shut for all this time; he or she may also find a spare portable heater for those gloomy winter months. The temperature of a room may not be to everyone's agreement: you think your room is a bit too fresh; a group of stroppy 14-year-old girls moan that they're baking...

It is not just temperature that can affect the comfort of a room. Take into account the other senses: is it easy to hear within the space? Or would students benefit from huddling in a little closer? Is the room well soundproofed or are you regularly interrupted by road drills, cars with big stereos or the din of the supply teacher's class next door? Are there any curious smells – the school canteen or the drains – that will distract students? I can recall hating entering the science block when I was at school. I was repulsed by the constant, lingering odour of pickling solution (connecting that smell with the sight of pickled frogs!) and needless to say, I never got very far with science!

Is the room easy on the eye? My previous classroom was painted in the most hideously bright, eye-stinging colours. After months of complaining (me and the students!) we had it painted a lovely, serene turquoise and immediately the atmo-sphere of the classroom became more relaxed. Is it easy for students to see the board, or are some of them having to crane their necks and twist their spines? Are those with poorer eye-sight in advantageous positions?

While it is not always possible to do anything about some of these issues, there may be little things you can do to make a difference. Importantly, when anticipating and dealing with classroom behaviour it is worth considering whether the conditions of the room may make an impact − if something is irritating you, it is just as likely to be irritating your students...

'Hot'-classing

If you are a supply teacher or unlucky enough not to have a fixed abode, make your life easier by being prepared.

1. Buy a big, sturdy bag.
2. Fill it with an A4-lined notepad; a plastic wallet full of stationery, including biros, pencils, colour pencils, board markers (different colours), rubber, pencil sharpeners (and spares), scissors, sticky tape, glue stick, sticky labels, stapler (and staples), paper clips, Tippex, ruler, compass, protractor, pocket calculator...
3. Emergency worksheet masters (quick activities for maths, literacy, word searches, crosswords, etc.).
4. Useful photocopies: detention slips, points charts, class lists, permission slips.
5. Diary, planner.

Hey presto! A classroom in a bag!

Part 5

Managing Behaviour

9 Helpful techniques...

One of the main reasons I am asked to get involved with a class or teacher is to look at the issue of challenging behaviour. Therefore, I am devoting the following section of the book to this subject. It is an issue that causes considerable concern among many echelons of society: the media, the government, the teaching unions, the parents, the public ... but the ones that do all the donkey work are, of course, the school staff. Managing behaviour is perhaps one of the hardest aspects of teaching, partly because it is secondary to the main purpose of the teacher's role ... which is surely to teach! Effective and meaningful behaviour management may need to be intensive, but time spent concentrating on this will mean time away from the curriculum. What do you do?

Unfortunately, there are no quick fixes to problematic classroom behaviour – or to the rigours of the learning process – these things require an investment of energy, time and consideration. The good news is that one gives rise to the other: get the lesson content right, and your students will be too 'on-task' to be enticed by undesirable activity. Get the behaviour control right, and your students will be more focused on their learning. If you balance good lessons and good behaviour simultaneously, you have the winning formula.

It can be a daunting prospect. If you are new to teaching, or have had unsuccessful ventures into behaviour management in the past, you are possibly quite apprehensive about it. Remember, you are not alone! Do not assume that you will never be able to cope with it – it may, indeed, be difficult to begin with, but any 'ageing' teacher will tell you that ability and confidence grows with experience. If you think it is something that just does not come naturally to you, bear in mind that effective behaviour management can be very formulaic. It is about working within a structure, being consistent and repetitive – about following a process. If you endeavour to understand and apply it in this way, you will be able to look past the idea that making kids behave is mystical talent belonging to a select few!

I have talked about the importance of being calm, firm, fair and consistent (Chapter 1). I now wish to emphasize three important skills that are common to effective teachers. If calm, firm, fair, etc. is to become your mantra, then these are to be your practical tools.

Eyes in the back of your head (being aware)

Why is it necessary?
Being aware of what is going on in your classroom enables you to stay ahead of your students. By being mindful of the activity that is taking place in all areas of the room, you will have tighter control of the experience. You will be able to spot off-task behaviour, keep track of student progress and ensure that no one is doing anything dangerous.

Limitations
Being vigilant can be demanding: you simply cannot be everywhere at once. It is difficult to keep track of the whole class while giving focused individual attention. It is especially difficult when working with primary students, who sit at tiny low desks – if you are down on their level, it is hard to get an overview of the rest of the room. Trying to combine individual student attention with awareness of the rest of class can be frustrating; you may have to interrupt your flow frequently.

Benefits
Being aware enables you to spot and deal with problems quickly and aids early intervention. Students may be deterred from getting involved with poor behaviour, feeling that it is too hard to 'get away' with: you always pick up on it. If they sense you are always on to them, students will be less likely to drift through a lesson without doing the work.

Aims

To keep students on-task. To undertake early inter-vention/ preventative intervention regarding behavioural issues. To keep track of pupil performance.

How to do it

1. When addressing the whole class, position yourself where you can have an overview of everyone: they see you, you see them.

2. Draw them in – remind them to face you, to look at you, and to listen. It can be helpful to use hand gestures to reinforce this (point to your eyes and then your ears).

3. If writing on the board, learn the art of facing sideways as you write – making it easier for you to keep one eye on the room.

4. Alternatively, place a mirror in a strategic position, and trick students into thinking you really do have eyes in the back of your head!

5. While students are getting on with individual activities, move around the class and make students feel they are being watched from all sides – be omnipresent.

6. If you are absorbed by one individual or have committed to working with a select group of students, ensure that you look up and scan the room whenever possible.

7. If you see or hear a problem, act on it. Unfortunately, this may mean interrupting what you are currently doing, but it will be more effective in the long run to 'nip it in the bud', than leave it to escalate further.

8. If the problem is persistent, avoid shouting across the room: go over and give a quiet, personal warning to the student(s), which will put them on the spot.

9. Ease the burden on yourself by encouraging students to help each other. If they see someone in need, can they provide the necessary assistance?

10. Likewise, encourage students to say no to wrongful temptation and to ignore/move away from silliness.

Growing an extra pair of hands (using support/teaching assistants)

As an ESBD teacher, I am used to working very closely with other staff. The effectiveness of our practice is reliant on good teamwork. I am familiar with the unbelievable benefits of working alongside good teaching assistants, but I have also had a few problematic experiences when sharing the responsibility of my students with others. Nowadays, many teachers have the opportunity to work with a teaching assistant(s), therefore I feel it is important to consider ways in which this working relationship can be made into a success.

Why is it necessary?

Classrooms may have more than one adult working in them, on either a permanent or temporary basis. Support assistants are often attached (not literally!) to an individual student, or group of students. In the primary class they may be available full or part time (depending on the need/statement requirement of the student). At secondary level, they will probably track a student through their lessons. Some assistants are attached to a whole class, and will be able to provide general classroom help. Another set of eyes, another pair of hands, another voice: having this extra support can be invaluable, but like all aspects of the classroom, it needs to be managed in order to maximize its effectiveness.

Limitations

Ineffective working relationships between teachers and teaching assistants can create more problems than they solve, but in the hectic bustle of the school day it can be difficult to find adequate time to put your heads together, discuss what has and will be going on in lessons, and consolidate your approach. Without some common understanding between you, confusion and inconsistency could arise: tension between staff will be noticed by students, who may merrily choose to take advantage of any vulnerable moments. Other problems include: staff undermining one another; issues of competitiveness/insecurity; lack of communication; fear of challenging one another (allowing issues to fester, which leads to resentment); lack of encouragement, praise and support; and contrasting/clashing methods of dealing with students.

Benefits

Having extra support can liberate your teaching, allowing you to get more out of all of your students. These days, support assistants are often well skilled, well trained and able to contribute in many ways (they are now being used as 'cheap' teaching staff). They may be able to take responsibility for a group of students, allowing you to concentrate on another group. They can provide the focused adult attention that some students will require in order to function in the classroom. They may also be able to organize differentiated work, keep restless students on-task, and calm any agitated individuals. If they are a regular fixture in your class, they will be able to help out with the display and organization of the room. Lastly, having some camaraderie can be fun: sharing the experience of a challenging class, being able to chat and laugh about it at the end of the day ... a great stress reliever.

Aims

To develop a unified, teamwork approach to classroom management. To provide mutual support and respect for each other's contributions. To establish efficient and productive ways of enabling all students to access the curriculum.

How to do it

1. If you regularly work with the same person, make time to discuss and review classroom approach and progress. Is it possible to schedule a brief weekly meeting?
2. If you work with someone on a daily basis, try to find a few minutes before the start of each day to run through the work, or any other issues.
3. After dealing with a difficult incident, take time to reflect on what worked/what did not work.
4. Be clear about how you expect the assistant to contribute in your classroom, and ensure that this reflects their job description and level of skill.

5. Encourage transparency between one another, enabling you both to communicate freely and openly about issues of concern.

6. Focus on developing a 'united front', finding ways of making your joint presence in the classroom consistent and strong: you back them up, they back you up. Hence the importance of good communication and consolidation of approaches.

7. Even if your classroom styles are very different, this can be used positively – accept difference, reflect on individual strengths and find ways of making it work. Often the contrast of strict and gentle personalities can be an effective combination (good cop, bad cop), as long as you are on the same side!

8. Be supportive, and look after one another – a cup of coffee and a chat can off-load stress and strengthen the relationship.

9. Show appreciation (encouraging words encourage positive action).

Becoming a mind-reader (understanding difficulties)

Why is it necessary?

Empathy is an important skill, both in terms of building positive relationships with your class (including the most difficult students) and preserving your sanity. If you are able to have some understanding of why certain children exhibit certain behaviours, you can separate this from your emotional response (anger, frustration, irritation). Empathy will increase your tolerance and may ultimately reduce your stress levels. It is not about making excuses for problematic behaviour, but about understanding the origins of it; which places you in an empowered position. If you know why something is happening, you will be able to address it more purposefully. If you are an understanding individual, your students will feel more secure and welcome in your class.

Limitations

With so many students in your responsibility, especially if you are a secondary school teacher, it is difficult to truly get to know each one (sometimes it is hard enough to simply remember their names!). When students are particularly or persistently foul it can wear you down. Some of them may try to test you to your limits – and although you can keep reminding yourself that they have 'issues', there may come a point when you have simply had enough...

Benefits

Empathy enables you to be more tolerant and to avoid taking things personally. It will help you to separate emotional reactions from practical, productive action. Empathy will also enable you to make informed decisions about how to deal with individuals, for example, some students may react very badly to shouting, others may become distressed if they think the class work is too hard – being aware of these things will help you to respond sensitively to students' needs, while giving you better insight into how to motivate them. Showing understanding will encourage your students to feel more supported and appreciated by you, which will lead to increased trust and respect. Expressing empathy towards a student that is distressed or angry will help them to calm down and communicate with you.

Aims

To develop an understanding of the needs and nature of your students and their behaviour. To use empathy in place of negative emotional reactions to students.

How to do it

1. Do your research and find out what you can about your students. Ensure that you are familiar with the needs of students with SEN. Look at statements, IEPS and reports and speak to the SENCO/SEN staff.
2. Be mindful of the difficult personal circumstances that some students may be struggling with: parental break up, bereavement, family illness, unstable home environments, neglect, financial hardship, etc.

3. Look out for signs of low self-esteem, depression and anxiety. Be careful not to compound these problems by being continually negative towards these students (however challenging their behaviour may be). Try to build a positive relationship with them and give plenty of encouragement.

4. When dealing with a distressed individual, acknowledge that you understand that they are upset and that you are willing to listen/help them. Give them the chance to explain their feelings and calm down before disciplining their behaviour.

5. Acknowledge the way your students may be feeling. Help them to name their emotions: sad, angry, disappointed, worried, annoyed, etc.

6. Take time to listen to what your students have to say. They themselves can give you the most valuable insight into what it is to be a youth in modern times.

10 Crowd control...

The effective management of challenging classroom behaviour can fall into two broad categories: dealing with whole class/groups of difficult students, and dealing with the individual. Do not think that one is necessarily easier than the other. Some teachers will roll their eyes with frustration whenever particular classes are mentioned: '9G? They're *unteachable*!'. But many will also testify that it takes just one difficult individual to disrupt everything, even if the rest of the group are quite tame.

In this section, I am going to concentrate on methods and approaches for dealing with group behaviour. These suggestions are based on problems I have seen occurring in the classes I have worked with. Issues include bullying in groups, coping with mixed ability classes, and dealing with 'mobs' (student groups that momentarily get out of hand). The most common of these issues, however, seems to be the 'off' class: the collective of students that, for one reason or another, cannot seem to function alongside members of the teaching profession, or each other. For me, these classes are very interesting to work with (perhaps not so for their long-suffering teacher!), for they present a multi-faceted challenge – an opportunity to explore the dynamics of the classroom and the interactions that take place within it.

The 'off' class

Sometimes you will hear staff talk about the 'funny' year. They do not mean funny *ha ha* – they mean funny as a euphemism for 'badly behaved', 'difficult' or 'there must have been something in the water the year they were born!' Every now and then, a year group comes up that seems to have more problems settling into education life than the average. The group gains notoriety as a dodgy bunch, which may then dog them for the rest of their schooling: 'Year 10? Oh yeah, don't worry – they're a shocking lot. Apparently they've been like it since Year 2 . . .'

Maybe the funny year group is just a myth pedalled by heads of year who want an excuse for not getting on top of the job, or perhaps there is something in it (the water, I mean) . . . either way, you will undoubtedly at some point have to teach members of such a sullied gang. If you stick firmly to the principles of good behaviour management, you should have no more problems than you would with any other year group – unless, of course, it *is* all to do with their star signs . . .

In this section I am going to look at ways to deal with a subdivision of the dodgy year group: the 'off' class. The class that fills you with dread every time you contemplate their cheeky little faces . . . You may face them once a week, you may have to take them for GCSE English, or you may indeed be their one guiding light, shackled to them at all times: their primary class teacher. In whichever capacity you encounter the 'off' class, it can be a physical, mental and emotional drain. And if you are really stuck in a rut, you may feel you simply cannot get anywhere with them. All is not lost. It could take some doing, but most groups of students can be shaken up and pulled back in.

If you feel you are struggling with such a class, the first thing you need to do is step back and take stock of the problem. What is actually happening during the lesson? Why is it happening? How is it being dealt with? Once you have gathered an understanding of the situation, you are better able to plan and implement strategies for managing it. Here are some suggestions.

Typical symptoms:

- Apathy related to learning, and lack of general motivation.
- Frequent interruptions.
- Disrespectful calling out/inappropriate banter between students.
- Frequent arguing and petty bickering – students easily distracted from work by a preoccupation with social/ antisocial interaction.

- Lack of respect for teacher authority: students that do not seem to take the classroom environment seriously.
- Deliberate ignorance or lack of awareness of classroom boundaries and conduct.
- Inability to cooperate with the teacher, and with each other: the group that does not gel.
- Repetitive problems – students fail to modify their behaviour for any sustained period, and continually return to 'bad habits'.
- Majority of the class are led into inappropriate activity by a minority.
- Over reliance on teacher to repeat instructions, and inability to get on with tasks independently: neediness.
- Disinterest in rewards and sanctions: nothing seems to have an effect.

Below are some possible causes for such behaviour.

Combination of personalities
Some classes can seem unbalanced (e.g. too many 'loud' or dominant individuals) and will not have a natural sense of cohesion.

Historical difficulties
Students that have remained together for several years (as primary classes, or as a tutor group) may become bored/impatient with one another's foibles. Although years together can help a class to bond, if they do not get on in the first place, longevity may just deepen the rift.

Association
If a class persistently causes problems, they can develop a reputation around, and even between, schools. Reputations can easily become self-fulfilling prophecies. Meek-looking 10-year-old girls often explain it to me: 'We're the naughtiest class in the school, miss. Is that why you've come to see us?'

External problems

Whatever goes on in the classroom can sometimes be perpetuated by what is going on outside of it. I have come across groups of students that constantly argue and cause problems for one another, only to find that their parents are exhibiting the same behaviours at the school gates – this can be particularly problematic in small, close communities.

Competition for 'top dog'

The social ladder is an inevitable part of any large collection of people – the classroom is no exception. Consider the pecking order of your students: maybe they fall into accepted ranking. Maybe there is constant competition for the top position: the coolest, hardest, smartest, most rebellious, etc. The challenge will increase if there are several forceful personalities in close proximity to one another.

Social life versus academic life

Social interaction is all part of the school experience, and usually rides politely alongside the other important part of the school experience: getting an education. Sometimes, however, the balance is upset and social concerns take over: who's been slagging off who becomes the predominant life force of the classroom, and that important SATs preparation is all but ignored.

Inappropriate work

If students are struggling to engage with the work, consider what is missing. Perhaps it is too challenging, too easy or just too plain boring. There is always a temptation with difficult groups to set straightforward, 'pin-them-to-the-desk' tasks that carry minimum risk factor; however, if these tasks are perceived by the students to be uninteresting, the plan will be counterproductive. One of the most effective ways to get students to stay on task is to give them something that grabs their attention.

Lack of teacher/class 'fit'

The powers that be should hopefully be taking care not to place newly qualified or less-confident teachers with the most challenging classes, but it does not always work out that way. Sometimes teacher and student personalities simply clash; it happens, we are human.

For the class that does not get on, an emphasis should be placed on activities that can help them to bond and learn to work together.

Here are some activities for classes with socialization problems.

Circle time

Suitable for younger students, this can involve the whole class or a group of students, and is based on talking activities that exercise listening skills, turn-taking, sharing, positive self-image, etc. It is a well-established programme – if you are not sure, look for books and other resources on the subject.

Problem solving tasks or challenges

Have them work in small groups or pairs (you choose the student combinations), and set them a task that requires team effort. For example:

1. Have them tie/untie giant rope knots (during which they have to negotiate and move around each other).
2. Get them to make a 'chair' out of old newspaper and string/sticky tape (the chair has to take your weight!) – this can be done as a competition between different groups; it is as fun as it is bonding.
3. Orienteering challenges. In which they have to follow a route via clues, either outside or within the school.

When setting activities of this kind, remember to be vigilant: the focus of the task is to get them to work 'together', you may need to monitor and support this process, otherwise it might not happen.

Team games

Use PE sessions as an opportunity to work on socialization. Emphasize turn-taking, fairness, encouraging others, and being a 'good sport'. Relate the success and achievement of different teams to the way in which they worked together and helped one another.

Group work

This is a more practical solution for the secondary classroom, where there is less flexibility within the curriculum. Incorporate group activities into your scheme of work, encouraging students to recognize each other's strengths and cooperate. Remember, it may be prudent for you to select the groups, and it will not necessarily be a matter of letting them get on with it – to make the most of the experience students may need to be guided into cooperating with one another, and supervised if difficulties arise.

Group projects

Sometimes it is beneficial to take the pressure off learning and get students involved in activities that can be relaxing and enjoyable, as well as relevant. Creative tasks such as poster design or model making can provide a calm, pleasant atmosphere in which to facilitate healthier group dynamics.

Drama activities, role-play and debate

These tasks can be fun, curriculum related and very helpful in getting students to bond. If it is not your thing, fear not. There is plenty of information available; alternatively, seek advice from your school drama department.

Socialization activities

Positive social skills stem from opportunities to learn and practise them. Setting up a breakfast club made an enormous difference in my ESBD classroom, in which students shared a meal together and developed table manners and polite, pleasant conversation. Many schools have breakfast clubs now, but you could consider recreating this in your own classroom occasionally (enabling you to focus specifically on the needs and relationships of your own students). Alternatively, consider using socialization activity as a reward: if students can show you they are able to cooperate and be helpful to one another throughout the term, they will be rewarded with a class party/outing.

For the class that has a negative self-image and lacks motivation, it is helpful to focus on ways of positively reframing this identity and raising expectations.

Here are some activities for raising class esteem.

PSHCE programmes on self-esteem
In my experience, PSHCE has often been an under-used subject. This is unfortunate, as there are many excellent (and easy to teach) resources regarding self-esteem and other relevant issues that are easily available.

Class discussion about ambition and goals
The value of education (both social and academic) is easily lost on some students. Encourage them to reflect on their lives (this can be relevant to both younger and older students) and what they want to achieve. How will they get there? What do they need? Who can help them? It might be fun – and powerful – to invite guest speakers ... the local celebrity footballer, perhaps?

Get involved with charity work
Build links with local community/charity projects. This may help students to recognize that they are capable of making a positive contribution to the world around them: that they are worthy individuals. It may also open up the pathway to volunteer work and outside interests: alternatives to kicking around the dusty streets for hours on end.

Set targets
Some students will benefit from having goals to work towards. At first, make them relatively easy to achieve; and heap on the praise, giving your students an initial boost of confidence.

Be positive yourself
Lead by example. If you are enthusiastic and optimistic about your students, they will want to please you. Even in the darkest, toughest of situations, positive thinking can be reinforced. If the

class is getting it all wrong, emphasize that you believe they can do better, rather than simply telling them it is not good enough. Imply that you will not give up on them until you see the results you know they should be getting.

Be generous with praise

Be purposeful and specific with praise. Praise is empty and meaningless if it does not impact on the intended recipient. Make it have an impact by being clear about who it is for and what it is for. 'I really appreciate the way you all listened carefully and took turns to speak in this lesson. It made the discussion very interesting and constructive' is more powerful than 'That was good'.

Get others to comment

If your class are beginning to make improvements, ask the head of year or another significant individual to casually pop their head in one lesson and pass comment: 'Wow! I'm really impressed by this class today!'

Here are some strategies to manage difficult whole classes.

Set/revisit rules and boundaries

Do not give up on clear boundaries – some individuals take a long time to adjust, but persistence pays. If necessary, go to the basics ('no talking when teacher is talking', 'do not get out of your seat without permission'). Select one or two key rules that will effect the overall classroom, and hammer these home. Keep it simple – get students used to following a few basic rules, before adding more.

Take control of seating plan

If you have not already done so, now might be the time. If you already have and it has not been beneficial, consider rearranging. You may want to change the entire structure of the desks (formal rows can have a calming influence on a rowdy lot), or you may want to mix up the student groups. Do not spend excessive hours agonizing over seating plans, however. Although playing puppet master over who sits next to who can be helpful, certain students will create problems wherever they sit.

Do not be afraid to move students around during lesson
I sometimes see teachers reissuing the same complaint/warning to the same chatty student five or more times during the course of one half-hour session. Who's not getting the point? Break the cycle early on by having the student move to another table or to an isolated desk. They may not like it, but that's just tough – next time they might think before opening their mouth!

Go strict on warnings and consequences
Think of yourself as an army major, and your students in boot camp. Make managing behaviour the focal point of your lessons for a few weeks. Tackle and follow up every little incident. Be ruthless, consistent and thorough. It may take up a considerable amount of classroom time, but it will be liberating in the long run.

Set work that makes them focus hard
Get their attention. Gear the subject towards their interests (e.g., an English project on advertising trainers or 'street-wear'). If students are unmotivated by the activity of class work itself, you will need to find other ways of luring them in.

Stop them
If the class is beginning to feel like a more powerful force than you are, stop the lesson. Regain control by interrupting their flow and pulling them back in. Have them sit silently for a few moments, or until the atmosphere is calmer, then explain why you chose to stop the lesson (too much noise, too many people out of their seats, etc). Allow them to resume activity, emphasizing your expectations. A complete, whole-class pause is more powerful than trying to constantly shout over the top.

Set whole-class consequences
Deal with whole-class disruptiveness by giving whole-class consequences (detention, keeping them in at break, etc.); but use this judiciously. Try to differentiate for those who have not

been causing problems, otherwise they may end up resenting you.

Be realistic!

Set them goals that are within their reach. Different classes improve and achieve at different rates and in different ways: a top set may have no problems knuckling down in silence – a lower set may have very different feelings towards class work. It is important to adjust your own expectations in order to feel positive about whatever class you are teaching – focus on improvement rather than perfection.

Dominant groups

I have suggested that in a peopled environment such as a classroom it is natural to have some kind of social hierarchy. Students will form friendship groups. There will be arguments, rivalry, make-ups and break-ups. Some individuals will be marginalized – others will try to dominate. All part of the normal school experience. But what happens when a group of individuals start to dominate the classroom so much that it interferes with the happiness and development of others?

When I am asked to make classroom observations I am often briefed about certain students that, according to the teacher, cause most of the problems – very often these students are all friends. While most of the class may be happy just to get on with the lesson, this group of characters have an agenda of their own. As individuals they may be cooperative and pleasant; but together they are trouble. Constantly trying to impress one another, influence each other's actions, and above all, hold on to status: we are the loudest/naughtiest/most popular/smartest gang in the class. Power ... we learn to want it from an early age.

Dominant groups of students, whether they are boys, girls or a mixture, can be intimidating for others in the class. While bullying may not necessarily be involved, a few pushy personalities can keep the shyer, less-confident members in the shade. It is important to look out for quieter students (even though your time may be taken up by the louder ones) and give them opportunities to contribute to classroom life. It may also be helpful to temper the interactions between particular groups by controlling the seating arrangements (however if you have not done this from the start, prepare to meet some resistance).

Bullying in gangs

Bullying of any sort should always be taken seriously. It is a widespread problem that needs careful consideration. The advice I give here is intended to provide general guidance, but it is only a beginning. Make sure you are familiar with your own school policy on the matter; know how to proceed and who to speak to if a problem arises.

Bullying in groups occurs in schools, ranging from skipping rope wars in the primary playground to the phenomenon of the teenage gang. There is no doubting the fact that it makes peoples' lives a misery. Unfortunately, it can also be hard to keep track of. A large amount of bullying takes place away from the watchful gaze of adults: break times, before/after school, on the bus, walking home. Sometimes the activity can be blatant, even violent; sometimes it is covert and subtle.

Wherever there are large groups of people there will be efforts to clamber on top of one another, such is human nature. Some individuals, for various reasons, seek to achieve this in ways that are detrimental to others. It is a complex issue that has no simple, straightforward solution. I have seen enough bullies and their victims in action to see that the problem is not just one of 'wrongness': it is a social, cultural and psychological minefield.

Bullying in groups (i.e., a group of students 'ganging' up against one or more individuals) perhaps stems from the need to belong and be accepted by others. In a primitive sense, it is about safety in numbers. Being part of the gang, doing what the gang does, is a way to secure your place in life. If one of the gang exhibits bullying behaviours, it may not take long for the others to join in.

The issue needs to be controlled by a strong anti-bullying policy and ethos, but this can take time to develop and embed itself in the consciousness of young people. As a teacher you have an important role to play in addressing the problem of bullies and their associates, but it does not rest entirely at your door (as some members of the public would suggest). School management, the media, the government, parents and the students themselves all have a role to play. To truly combat bullying, everyone has to take ownership of the situation.

Be vigilant

You will not always be told, or be aware, that something is going on. Watch out for signs of bullying behaviour in the classroom. This can be: isolation of individuals; arguments and squabbles; unkind remarks; sudden changes in friendship groups; changes in student attitude; and individuals becoming withdrawn, sullen or tearful, not wanting to take part in activities or playtimes. If you have concerns, break duty may be a helpful opportunity to see more behaviour. Talk to other staff and find out if they have noticed anything; likewise, alert them to any concerns you have about members of their tutor group/ class.

Show that you are aware

A victim of bullying will not necessarily speak out about their experience. You need to find a way of reassuring the victim that you are aware of the problem and are able to help, without making them feel unsafe, uncomfortable or ashamed. Speak to them privately and broach the subject gently.

Seek support

It may be necessary to call in the support and advice of other members of staff (form tutor, head of year, learning mentor, school counsellor, etc.). They can help you to make informed decisions about how to tackle the problem. Sharing information will also increase awareness of the situation, enabling staff to act swiftly and efficiently.

Be discreet

Be careful when addressing problems of bullying with the whole class. While it is important to be transparent about what bullying is and how unacceptable it is, victims should not be put in a position where they feel exposed or have unnecessary attention drawn to them in front of their perpetrators. It may lead to further problems.

Find out who is involved and who the ringleaders are

The victim(s) and other members of the class may be able to provide names, if you yourself are not sure. You may need to speak to the bullies themselves before you can establish a clear picture. Speak to students individually before addressing them as a group.

Follow school policy guidelines

Some schools have zero tolerance to bullying. Some will operate a 'three strikes and you're out' system. Others will be more compromising. Most schools will require the involvement of parents in some way.

Monitor the situation

Even if it appears that a bullying incident has been successfully dealt with, it could quickly resurface, or simply be pushed towards more covert activity. For many, bullying is rarely a one-off experience (in terms of both giving and receiving). It can be ongoing and, sadly, it can become character defining.

Look after the victims

Ensure that victims of bullying receive the guidance and comfort they need. Do they have a network of friends? If not, are there ways of facilitating support for them by a 'circle of friends', peer mentoring, 'buddy' systems, a change of class, or getting them involved in clubs and activities? How is their emotional state of mind? Should they be referred to a youth counselling service or self-esteem group? Are they coping with class work?

Look after the bullies

People do not bully because they are inherently evil. They are drawn into it for all sorts of reasons: peer pressure, insecurity, jealousy, acting out personal anger, underlying feelings of inadequacy, or because they themselves are being bullied.

Unless these reasons are addressed, bullying behaviour will keep recurring. Look at ways of raising the self-esteem of the bully, and encouraging them to reflect on how their behaviour affects others. Bullies may benefit from counselling, or participation in anger management/self-esteem groups.

Mixed-ability classes

It is not uncommon to have a broad range of ability in one class – ranging from the gifted and talented to those with severe/ moderate learning needs. Even in subjects that are streamed, there may be significant difference between the strongest and weakest students in the class. Add to this the idea that teachers should ensure they are catering for a range of learning styles, that some students may not have English as a first language, that others bring with them that trait we all love so much: behavioural difficulties ... a complete melting pot! This section deals with how to tackle the mixed ability group, and keep your sanity at the same time.

Use your assistants (if you have them)
Teaching assistants can play a key role in managing the learning of so many different individuals. They will be able to provide focused support to students with SEN (dealing with either one or several individuals at a time), and can assist in reading, differentiating tasks and preparing resources. More experienced staff may be able to lead a larger group of students, while you concentrate on another one.

Consider seating arrangements
Some teachers choose to seat their students by ability – having a specific table for the most able, and another for the least able. This may seem somewhat elitist, but it does make life easier when you are setting work. If the brightest students are together, they will be able to pace and motivate one another. If less able students are seated together, staff will be able to monitor and address their needs more easily. However, this arrangement is flawed: weaker students will not be able to have their learning enriched by working alongside more able individuals, and if

behavioural problems are involved the spread of students may need to be reassessed.

Spread your attention
Consider how you can share out your attention so that everyone benefits – it is perhaps one of the hardest things a teacher has to do. Many a staff member has nearly snapped through the frustration of having their attention stretched in ten different directions. First of all, accept – and encourage your students to accept – that you cannot be everything to all people at once. Set up clear guidelines for how students are to gain your attention (no calling out, no getting up and wandering after the teacher like a string of ducklings, no waggling pieces of paper in front of the teacher's nose, no grabbing at their clothes, no standing on the desk ...) and then make sure you are frequently scanning the whole classroom, as well as working with individuals and groups.

Rotate the intensity of activities
Allow yourself opportunities to give focused attention to students working at different levels, by rotating the difficulty of tasks. When you set a task that pushes your more able students, give weaker ones something that they are suitably able to complete independently, and vice versa. This will enable you to concentrate on working with one group, while the others are (hopefully) able to cope on their own.

Work to the pace of the average student
Find out where the majority of students are at, and pitch your general teaching to that level. This way, most of the class will be well catered for, and you will have a clear barometer of student progress. Tasks can be differentiated from this level: simplify for weaker students, complicate for stronger ones – allow them the flexibility to move on, or hold back.

Differentiate
Providing differentiated tasks is one of the most important aspects of making the most of a class with mixed ability. Tips

and ideas for doing this successfully and easily were provided in
Part Two: Lesson Structure and Content.

Work with groups
Consider dividing the class into three or four working groups
for individual tasks, and alternate your attention between these
groups. If you have support staff they could take the responsibility for one of the groups. For example: teaching assistant
with Group A, you work with Group B, and Group C works
independently (remember to alternate the groups next lesson),
allowing a number of different activities to be undertaken at
once – very productive. It also enables you to stream students
within the classroom, giving you the chance to focus your
attention on a smaller number of individuals at a time. Making
it work, however, requires good organizational skills and
careful preparation.

Use plenty of visual cues
Make use of visual resources, vocabulary lists and handouts,
providing continuous opportunities for learning to be reinforced. For instance, those that may struggle to listen to
information may pick up key words if they are already written
on the board.

Set targets for different levels
Use differentiated target setting as a way of encouraging individuals within mixed ability classes. These targets can address
the progress of groups/tables of students – stretch the able ones,
and motivate the weaker ones.

Look out for signs of dissatisfaction
If work is too easy or too hard, students will usually give away
telltale signs, although they may not always admit to having
problems. If students seem to be uncharacteristically disengaged
or bored, they perhaps need more challenge. If, on the other
hand, they are producing incomplete work, making excuses or
constantly struggling to keep up, the level may be too high.
Watch out, however, for those that try to call your bluff;

claiming that work is too hard/too easy, in order to have an easier time/deny their weakness.

Remember to challenge weaker students as well

Although they may be achieving and progressing at a much slower rate, low-level students also need to be pushed and challenged, otherwise they may become demoralized and bored. Balance challenge with accessibility.

Taming a mob

It is the moment that any teacher dreads: a group of students that you cannot get control of. Sometimes it feels as though the potential is there on a daily basis (see 'The "off" class', p. 97), sometimes it happens circumstantially – a fight suddenly erupts or unstoppable banter takes over. Battling for classroom control is not just something that newly qualified teachers struggle with; it can happen to anyone at any point in their career. The skill lies in learning how to regain control.

Firm, consistent general behaviour management will make these situations less likely to occur in the first place. If students know what to expect from you, and what you expect from them, they will be more wary of pushing the boundaries. If they have respect for you and your approach to the classroom, they will follow your instructions without too much fuss. There are, however, some individuals out there who will constantly try to explore the limits of your patience. And if they are the kind that are able to whip other members of the class into a frenzy, you will know just how much effort it can take to stay on top. Teachers that have infrequent contact with their classes, or perhaps do supply work, may also experience difficulties getting and keeping control of challenging groups of students, as they do not have the benefits of an established relationship with the class.

Here are some guidelines on how to confront and manage a group of students that are going too far too quickly. Before you even think about telling them off, you need to get them to listen to what you are saying. This is easier said than done – if they are locked into an argument or banter between themselves, you will be low on their list of priorities. I have often watched teachers yelling at students: 'If you don't stop talking and calling out, you'll all be in detention!' hoping that the threat of a consequence will get them to behave. I have also watched the reaction of these students ... they could not care less. They are not hearing what the teacher is trying to say; they are enjoying themselves too much. The more distressed the teacher becomes, the more they take advantage. Your priority is to get them to stop interacting with one another and start interacting with you. Avoid making threats and inflammatory remarks that may just escalate the problem further, and focus on reclaiming the attention of these individuals. This can be done in different ways.

Physical presence
Step among the problem. Try to be a barrier between students communicating with one another. Intervene by approaching one of the problematic students, getting down on their level and talking quietly and directly to him/her: 'Stop. You need to look at me. Pay attention. You need to calm down.' Be firm and persistent. It is more distracting to speak intimately to a student, than to shout at them from afar.

Vocal distraction
Use your voice, or another loud sound (a bell/buzzer/hand clap), to shock students into paying attention. A short, sharp noise will do this more effectively than a long nag about poor standards of behaviour – if you wish to set consequences this can be done once the situation has settled.

Once you have the attention of the students (or at least some of them) you need to act quickly in order to hold on to that attention, and to prevent the situation from slipping away from you again. Divide and rule! The next aim, therefore, is to break up the group that is causing the problem and come between them and their audience.

Remove the student

This is usually the most effective way of putting a stop to classroom antics. If you pick the right student (i.e., the main protagonist) you will not only separate them from their pals, but you will get them away from the audience they are trying to amuse. Be watchful of students that may continue to entertain the class once they have been sent out: pulling faces at the window and other such mature, dignified behaviour.

Separate key protagonists

Alternatively, you may consider separating individuals within the classroom space − having them sit in far corners − with the advantage that you can keep an eye on them all. However, this may be of little use if they are prone to hollering across the room at one another.

Remove the audience

If efforts to tame an unruly few are not getting very far, the answer may be to remove the oxygen of publicity − take the class elsewhere and leave them to it! Obviously, this presents a logistical nightmare: where do you take 25 confused students and how do you monitor the ones that are left? It can, however, be a powerful last resort. If you decide to do this, do it calmly − emphasize a 'we're quite bored of you now, so we're going to go somewhere else and do something nice ... it's a shame for you' attitude, otherwise they may feel they have 'won'.

Support the process of conquering the mob by praising and giving positive attention to those who are doing, or trying to do, the right thing − particularly those who are ignoring attempts to get them to join the 'dark side'! Reinforcing helpful behaviour will encourage others not to get caught up in the silliness.

11 Dealing with individuals...

Having looked at ways to tackle tricky group situations, I will now focus on how to deal with individual students. When I am making observations in schools, it is often because I have been asked to look at the behaviour of a particular child – very often, one individual is able to cause a considerably large headache for the teacher. The phrase I seem to hear most commonly is: 'I've tried everything – I just don't know what to do anymore.'

If a teacher is having to spend an excessive amount of time dealing with one child, they may grow weary and resentful. They may begin to feel that the rest of the class are missing opportunities and not being pushed as hard as they could be: further frustration. If the student in question is failing to respond to techniques of behaviour management (as is often the case), the problems will be compounded. The teacher may feel as though they are failing, which will damage their morale and affect their ability to cope with the rest of the job...

I sincerely hope this is not a familiar sounding pattern of events to any of you, however, with the uptake of *inclusion* it has increasing potential to be so. Whether we agree with the principle or not, the inclusion of students with SEN into the mainstream environment is having a profound affect on school communities. For all of its many positives, there are undeniable challenges. The toughest of these seems to be the integration of students with – yes, you've guessed it – emotional, social and behavioural difficulties (ESBD).

The management of students with ESBD will never be straightforward. Success (which can often be tenuous) is dependent upon knowing the individual well, understanding how they affect and are affected by their circumstances, and on building a relationship of trust and tolerance – a relationship that takes many months to form. The majority of ESBD students need specialized and intensive input in order to function within the orderly, rigorous environment of the classroom. There is a great need for flexibility: the space to make exceptions, to give second chances and to concentrate on the absolute basics. In reality this can be difficult to provide – where there is lack of resources, lack of training and lack of time. Few mainstream classroom teachers could consistently provide the level of support required by some ESBD individuals – not through want of trying – but because it simply is not possible within the context of whole-class need.

I have heard many competent classroom teachers claim they have run out of ideas, options and energy through battling to manage certain students. The first piece of advice I give them is to step back, relax and accept the situation. Some of us have a tendency to believe that if a student is constantly misbehaving, then we are not doing our job well enough – but young people misbehave for all sorts of profound and complex reasons. (No one would question it if the child had a clinically defined condition, such as autism or ADHD.) A child with behavioural problems *has behavioural problems*: in other words, they will naturally present more challenge than the average student. Pressuring yourself into feeling that you have to lick them into 'perfect' behavioural shape, in line with the rest of the students, is helping no one. Accept that these individuals will prove difficult from time to time, but that this, in no way, undermines your teaching abilities.

Of course, not every student that creates difficulties in the classroom will have a statement of SEN (and not all SEN students will create difficulties). This means there are a significant number of students out there who are willing and able to be challenging in the classroom, without recourse to additional support or official acknowledgement of need. Difficult behaviour varies in its intensity, nature and origins – from 'naughty' to 'disturbed'.

Understandably, the concern is that difficult classroom behaviour from one individual compromises the progress and experience of other students. You may feel that if you cannot tame the issue, it will destroy the rest of your good work. There is no magic fix for this conundrum. For the sake of your personal sanity, it is perhaps a matter of learning to work *with* the problem, rather than against it: fitting your expectations around the students you have been given, rather than expecting students to fit your idea of a successful class. While it is important for a teacher to have high expectations of their students, these expectations need to be realistic.

The following section is designed to provide accessible, straightforward guidance on how to recognize and deal with a variety of problematic student 'types'. I have provided fictional student profiles to help highlight the kind of issues I am examining, and have listed some strategy suggestions. The selection of 'types' I provide here is by no means exhaustive, but perhaps represents some of the more common problems that can surface within the classroom.

Withdrawn students

Profile

Alex is 8 years old. She moved to the area last year, and is therefore relatively new to the school. However, she has made very little progress in terms of settling in. By now you feel she should have established friendship groups, or at least be interacting with other members of the class – she is doing neither. The rest of the students pay little attention to her, and seem to talk about her rather than to her, although there is no evidence of bullying. At break times she tends to wander around on her own. Her academic progress is slow, though you feel she is capable of much more. She never contributes to class discussion, and you have found it difficult to make informal conversation with her – she is usually monosyllabic. She is nervous and often appears to be in a daydream. You have spoken to her mother about your concerns, and her mother has suggested that it is 'just a phase': that Alex has been unhappy about some of the changes in her life (parents' divorce, moving house), and will probably get back on track in her own time.

Key concerns
- Student has not settled in her new school.
- Student does not interact with others.
- Student is not making adequate progress with work.
- Student is generally uncommunicative with adults as well as children.
- Student may have poor levels of concentration.
- There may be underlying emotional issues and anxiety.
- Student's mother may not be fully acknowledging the problem.

The problem

Withdrawn students may not be problematic in a disruptive sense, therefore it can be easy to overlook them: they are unlikely to draw attention to themselves in the way more boisterous students would. However, as the profile suggests, if a young person is in a withdrawn state they may not be engaging socially or academically, and this may impede their overall progress. Unusually withdrawn behaviour at a young age could mean the student is failing to develop important social skills.

Excessive quietness and introspection can be a manifestation of underlying emotional issues. Sometimes the origin of these problems can be obvious, such as parental conflict or unwelcome change. Sometimes the underlying reasons are harder to fathom, and may require further intervention. Depression, anxiety, and low self-esteem are likely to play a significant role.

There are, of course, those students that are naturally quiet and timid – it is important to recognize the difference between a happy shy student and unhappy one. It is also important to remember that withdrawn behaviour can be an indication that the child is being bullied – this may need to be addressed.

Strategies
- Try to develop a relationship between yourself and the student in order to establish a line of communication and build trust. Start with simple things (their interests: music, sport, etc.) and allow the bond to grow steadily – placing too much pressure may frighten them away.
- Encourage contribution in class, but avoid 'picking on'

the student or drawing excessive attention to them – this could be unpleasant for them. It may be helpful to place less emphasis on 'hands up' class discussion. Select students yourself, allowing you more control over who contributes but without singling out individuals.

- Praise the student if they make contributions in class, but consider doing this discreetly so as not to cause embarrassment.
- Motivate the student academically by setting small targets, and giving praise when they have been achieved. Ensure that the student fully understands the work that has been set – depression can cause lapses in concentration.
- Create small-scale socialization opportunities, such as group/pair work in which students have to have discussion – less intimidating than talking in front of a large group of people.
- Ask a few trusted members of the class to 'befriend' the student at break times, and help him/her to integrate with others. This can be very effective, but may need some monitoring.
- Look for ways to raise the student's self-esteem: for example, encourage them to participate in clubs or activities that interest them. Be enthusiastic about their work, and emphasize the positives.
- Consult with other staff – they will be able to provide continuity of support for the student around the school.
- Raise concerns with parents/guardians, who could have further insight into the child's difficulties, and may able to help/benefit from your help.
- Having discussed your concerns with other relevant parties, decide together whether it is necessary to seek further support and intervention for the student, such as therapeutic input.

Attention seekers

Profile
Danny is 12 years old. He is a likeable individual, but has a tendency to show off and distract the rest of the class. He finds

it difficult to handle listening to the teacher, and will often interrupt or call out inappropriately. He tries to say and do things that will make other students laugh, and will often make silly noises or answer back in a cocky but jocular fashion. Sometimes the class find him amusing; sometimes they are fed up with him. If he is not making the impact he desires, he will push it even further. His behaviour will become increasingly silly and disruptive, until he is sent out of the classroom. He will apologize for his actions, but often insincerely – sometimes you sense he is trying to manipulate you into allowing him back into the classroom. He does not appear to take much seriously. His academic ability is slightly below average, and he needs continuous reminders to stay focused during individual work.

Key concerns
- Student is preoccupied with being 'liked'.
- Student has poor listening skills.
- Student may lack self-control, and does not recognize boundaries of inappropriateness.
- Student frequently disturbs the rest of the class.
- Student is failing to learn from his own behaviour – does not seem motivated to make genuine changes.
- Student is not making satisfactory academic progress.
- Student absorbs too much teacher time.

The problem
Students like Danny are a common feature of many classrooms. The frustration is perhaps not so much in what they do, but how they fail to stop doing what they do. It is very hard to make changes in students whose behaviours define their personalities. It is likely that Danny's burning desire to be the centre of attention manifested itself a long time ago. He now has the identity of class clown/joker/entertainer to live up to.

He is obviously seeking some kind of satisfaction from his antics, which overrides his understanding of how to behave in a learning environment. The fact that the class sometimes enjoy what he does is temporarily fulfilling this need. When they are bored of him, he will go to new lengths in order to reclaim their appreciation. Beneath the bravado, Danny is a very insecure individual.

Attention-seeking behaviour can be frustrating for the teacher, who is obliged to keep distractions to a minimum and may therefore spend a considerable amount of time intervening. There is a danger that some students will start to seek *any* attention (including negative reactions, such as being told off) in order to feel validated – 'naughty' behaviour becomes a means to an end. It can be difficult to resolve: the roots of the issue will probably lie somewhere far beyond the school gates.

Strategies

- Develop a positive relationship with the student. Take an interest in them that goes beyond having to tell them off; for example, make an effort to chat informally with them after the lesson – this may give them the confidence to just be themselves in your classroom.
- Model positive ways of gaining attention. Give your class attention for the right reasons, and be specific about what it is that they are doing right: 'Well done Susan – I'm going to come over to your desk now, because I'm really pleased with the way you are working so carefully...'
- Avoid dramatic reactions to negative attention seeking behaviour. Use indifference rather than anger: 'That behaviour really doesn't interest me ... settle down and get on with your work please.'
- Be direct. Tell the student what you would like to see them doing: 'I'm looking forward to hearing your contributions to the lesson today – don't forget to put your hand up though.' Praise them when they do it right, ensuring that positive behaviour is reinforced (good attention for good reasons).
- Use an individualized targets/points chart to encourage the student to make an effort to reduce the amount of calling-out or distracting behaviour.
- Seat loud attention-seeking students at the back of the class, where they are less visible to the rest of the class, and therefore less likely to distract them.
- Encourage other members of the class to ignore silly, disruptive behaviour. Always praise them for doing this – it is not easy.

- Turn negative attention-seeking on its head. If a student is making silly interruptions, point out that they have obviously got a lot to say for themselves ... so what do *they* think about Pythagoras' Theorum? Put them on the spot, where they need to use the vocalism constructively.
- Find ways of enabling the student to channel their love of attention. They may well excel in activities such as drama, role-play and debate. Encourage them to use their energy wisely, and turn it into a skill.

Students that are 'full-of-beans'

Profile

Leon is 6. He is currently under assessment for attention deficit disorder. He exhibits many of the traits associated with the condition, but most noticeable is his relentless restlessness. He continuously fidgets, is frequently out of his seat and cannot concentrate for any length of time. He has little self-control over these issues, although he responds when told off (however, improvements are always short-lived). Leon's parents report similar behaviour at home, and are finding him very difficult to manage. Recently, he has been bothering other students during carpet time. When they are sat on the floor, he wriggles about and sometimes prods and provokes them. Often you turn around to find that he has done something reckless; for example, left taps running in a blocked sink, or pulled all of the coats from their pegs. You feel that he is a liability when left unattended. He finds it difficult to follow instructions and settle down to tasks. In short, he exhausts you!

Key concerns

- Assessment can be a long process: you are currently receiving no additional support for this student.
- Student's restlessness is impeding his access to learning and development.
- Student lacks self-control and self-awareness.
- Student's behaviour can be reckless, and at times unsafe.
- Student seems to need constant monitoring.
- Behaviour is beginning to aggravate other students.
- Student's constant fidgeting distracts others.

The problem

Leon's behaviour places considerable demands on those responsible for him. It seems that many people having to deal with a child exhibiting similar problems would pin their hopes on explaining the behaviour through the diagnosis of ADD/ADHD, but having an accurate medical diagnosis is only a start. ADD/ADHD is a difficult disorder to manage, requiring intense effort, patience and determination from those involved.

The fact that Leon's actions are relentless is probably one of the most frustrating aspects of the problem – not just for you, but for him too. He may not necessarily be able to help doing what he does; being repeatedly told off for it will only compound his frustrations. You, however, have to be able to draw a clear line between what you will and will not tolerate in order to maintain a clear sense of boundaries amidst the rest of the class. You also have to take account of any behaviour that may be distracting/disruptive for them.

The vigilance required to keep track of Leon's antics is difficult to provide in a busy, crowded classroom. The support of a teaching assistant could make a considerable difference, but if this is in limited supply (as it often seems to be), the benefits will only go so far for a student that needs constant refocusing.

Strategies

- Liaise with the others. Work as closely alongside other people responsible for the child as you can. If behaviour management strategies can be applied as consistently as possible, the chance of the child getting the idea increases. Communicate with the child's parents/guardians frequently, and compare your approaches to the child's actions. Consider ways in which you can support one another.
- Ask to be kept informed. Make sure you know what is going on in terms of the child's assessment and programme of care. It is very likely that you will be asked to make a contribution during the assessment process. If a diagnosis has been made, it is important that you are aware of how it is being treated and whether medication is being prescribed. You should also be alerted to any subsequent

changes in medication, as this may have a dramatic effect on the child's behaviour.

- Develop empathy. It is helpful – for your own sanity – that you endeavour to understand that a child with an attention/conduct disorder may not always be able to control what they do. Distance yourself from the idea that the child is conspiring to get on your nerves. Ensure that this understanding is communicated to the child, so as to protect their self-esteem.

- Rewards/points chart. For a child that struggles to control their actions, it is important to focus on positive reinforcement of the right behaviour, rather than constant telling off for wrong. A points chart is a useful way to promote and monitor their achievements, and provides a tangible, visual reference for the student.

- Combat the distraction of fidgety behaviours by working *with* the problem. If the child has a tendency to 'fiddle', give them something quiet to fiddle with – a square of fabric or a piece of ribbon. Encourage them to use this in place of pencil tapping, ruler snapping, finger drumming and other such irritating habits!

- For younger students that are restless during carpet time or assembly, provide a 'sitting spot': a coloured disk that they have to stay on (this could be permanently stuck in a certain strategic location), helping them to remember to stay in one place.

- Develop visual or auditory cues for the student: ways to signify that they need to refocus or stop what they are doing. These cues (such as a hand signal, a tap on the shoulder, or even a code word) can represent a friendlier alternative to nagging or telling off, and will draw less unwanted attention to the child's behaviour.

- Encourage peer support. Make sure other students in the class have some level of understanding of ADD/ADHD so that they are able to recognize why the student may be having certain difficulties. If necessary, give them some guidance on how to relate or react to the student if problems arise.

- Use targets to motivate the student and encourage progression.
- Avoid extended periods of time in which the student has to sit and listen; or if this cannot be helped, make allowance for the student to get on with a quiet activity (for example, a colouring-in sheet or word search), while you address the class.
- When setting individual work, provide a breakdown of the tasks that need to be done, enabling the student (whose ability to concentrate will be limited) to complete it in smaller, more manageable steps; and assisting them in terms of sequencing their efforts.
- Keep instructions simple and clear. Repeat them several times, in order to reinforce what needs to be done – it can be difficult for a child with ADD to retain information.
- Make use of a quiet area/time-out chair, in which the child can go if they (or you) feel they are becoming over-excited and in need of some personal space to calm down. This can be suitable for older students as well as younger ones, as it encourages them to develop a responsibility for managing their own behaviour.
- Give the student as much outlet for their energy as possible. It is not a good idea to 'punish' an ADD student by denying them their break time ... forcing them to miss an opportunity to run around and exert themselves may mean trouble later in the day!

The bad socialite

Profile

Dean is 10. He has had ongoing difficulties integrating with other students since Reception. He is a bright, well-motivated student and is generally polite and cooperative when relating to adults. He struggles to emulate this success when dealing with his peers. He has not formed any meaningful friendship groups, but is not what you would describe as a 'loner'. He tends to get involved with other children, but in ways that antagonize them. He seems to have an immature sense of social skills and awareness. He will deliberately say things to upset or aggravate members of the class and has, on several occasions, behaved quite aggressively. He is often involved with fights. When reproached for his actions he becomes surly and defensive, and avoids acknowledging why his behaviour hurts others. He has a competitive streak and will try to dominate students during break-time football games or group activities. This will often lead to arguments. Although there have been several attempts to raise these concerns with Dean's parents, little ever comes of it – they are unreliable and somewhat dismissive.

Key concerns
- Student lacks social awareness.
- Student has shown limited capacity to develop social skills so far.
- Student may be seeking to interact with others, but does it in inappropriate, ineffective ways.
- Student may have low self-esteem, or feel a need to prove himself.
- If student's aggressive behaviour continues he may be at risk of exclusion.
- Student finds it difficult to apologize or take responsibility for his behaviour.
- Engaging consistent parental support is difficult.

The problem
Cases like Dean's are difficult to tackle. When social problems have developed and manifested over considerable time (in this case, Dean's entire childhood), they become harder to unravel – hence the value of *early intervention*. The reasons for his social difficulties are unclear, but the unsupportive attitude of his parents is perhaps a hint of familial disharmony. Encouraging a young person to make changes in their behaviour can be a frustrating process if the work is not upheld in their home environment.

The rest of the class have probably developed a firm understanding of what young Dean is 'like' so will naturally tend to keep their distance. Unfortunately, this creates little opening for Dean to make changes. Unless he develops a more effective social and emotional vocabulary, and is given the chance to try this out, he will continue to rely on less appropriate methods of making connections with others.

It seems that Dean overcompensates for his inability to form satisfying social relationships by proving himself in other ways – his competitiveness and his urge to be a dominant, if unpopular, figure. As an able student, it is of considerable concern that he may jeopardize his academic development because of his aggression. Additionally, as a student about to enter secondary school, if he is struggling to cope with the social activity of a stable primary environment, what will become of him in a large secondary?

Strategies

- Model good social skills. If a student has struggled to pick up on general social habits, it may be helpful to give them some concrete examples to learn from. Next time there is a problem, intervene and than act out/demonstrate how the student could have reacted better.
- Reinforce through praise. When the student gets it right, show your appreciation: 'I really liked the way you helped Vicky with her maths . . . that was very thoughtful of you.' Encourage them to feel positive about being helpful/polite/respectful.
- Whole-class work on communication skills. Use PSHCE activities to look at effective ways of respecting each other's feelings and communicating with one another. Getting the whole class involved will reduce the pressure on the individual student, thus they are less likely to feel that they are the one that always gets it wrong.
- Role-play activities. Use scenario based role-play/drama to explore ways of solving disputes and to help students find alternatives to arguing and fighting. As a small group activity, role-play can also be a useful time for the student to work on positive social interaction.
- Encourage others to walk away. Give the rest of the class some support and guidance on how to cope with the student's inappropriate behaviour: to ignore, to avoid answering back, to speak to an adult, to move away. Be careful not to alienate the student, however.

- Use supervised play to model good practice. If competitiveness is a problem, the student may benefit from taking part in supervised lunchtime activities (if such luxury is available), where their reactions can be more closely monitored. Encourage game-play that does not have a win/lose outcome, or has a focus on achieving personal bests. Sport can be an excellent vehicle through which to teach a variety of social skills: self-control, fairness, self-esteem, taking turns, encouraging others and positive attitude. It is also a subject that many young people are keen to engage with.
- Anger management. The student may benefit from some focused time to reflect on his feelings and his behaviour, and to be given a non-judgemental arena in which to voice himself. Anger management courses have a good track record in helping young people to deal with their feelings.
- Raise the student's self-esteem. Encourage the student to identify and make use of their strengths. In this case, he is bright and hard working. As an outgoing, dominant character he may also be good at organizing others. How can he use these skills positively? Perhaps he could be responsible for helping others with their work, or becoming a peer mentor to a group of younger students.

Reluctant workers

Profile

Kieran is 15. His attendance at school has become increasingly erratic, and he is generally disinterested in his studies. He is a student of average ability, but at this rate will do very poorly in his forthcoming exams. He is behind on his coursework, and has repeatedly failed to hand in homeworks and complete assignments. Teachers across the curriculum have expressed their concerns about him. He does, however, have a positive attitude towards design and technology. His form tutor has repeatedly tried to address the problem, but Kieran's response is casual and unbothered. His behaviour in class is rarely a problem, but he is prone to bunking off. He is often found hanging around corridors with a group of like-minded 'chums'; they can be cocky and rude when approached by staff.

Key concerns
- Student is failing to achieve.
- Student has poor attendance.
- Student has fallen behind significantly, and has now jeopardized exam success.
- Student is disengaged from learning.
- Student is unwilling to make an effort to get on top of the situation.
- Student is becoming disaffected around school, and is surrounded by inappropriate peer influences.

The problem
There are of thousands of Kierans out there. Students that coast along, steadily making progress and set for personal success – and then just as crunch time starts to draw near, they slip away. Disengagement with the learning environment is one of the tragedies of the education world. It is even more frustrating when the student in question has previously shown good potential.

For Kieran, the problem has already done its damage – although he himself has avoided identifying with the consequences of this. Apathy over the last year has led to limited amounts of coursework and scant subject knowledge; no amount of cramming (if he bothers to do any) will redress this adequately.

The biggest hurdle is getting him motivated. In order to motivate a person, it is helpful to know what makes them tick. Evidently, Kieran has an interest in design and technology – this could be a key to revitalizing his efforts. But while classroom learning is in competition with social distractions, the battle may be hard to win. Kieran's fate is almost sealed: underachiever.

Strategies
- Tackle it early. Early intervention is crucial. The longer a student is able to sit back, the further they will fall behind –

making it harder to get back on top in the long run. As soon as you pick up on signs of apathy or a reluctance to produce satisfactory work, start investigating the situation.

- Identify causes. The reasons why a child may become disengaged with learning are varied. It may be as simple as them finding the work too difficult, but frightened to admit it; or the origins maybe more complex, such as difficult home circumstances, depression or peer pressure. If you can find reasons why the student is losing their way, you are much more likely to find the solutions.
- Engage the parents/carers. If you can complement your efforts with support and encouragement from the home, the pressure to learn and achieve will be more stable. For younger students, it is helpful to encourage parents to get involved with their children's homework and reading. A home/school liaison report can be an effective way of monitoring the student's efforts. I know of one parent who used to sit in lessons with her child, in order to police his work! This is not, however, a practice I would necessarily recommend – over pushy parents can some-times be the root of the problem.
- Encourage students to reflect on their futures, and why achievement in school may help them get to where they want to be. Although they tend to get it rammed down their throats, hearing it from the right people (i.e., people they respect and admire) can be a potent way of con-veying the message. Invite guest speakers to give motivational talks. There are some willing sports person-alities and pop stars out there!
- Use attendance at homework clubs/revision classes as a consequence for not handing in work. If the student is failing to produce the goods in their own time, take control of that time. Instead of setting aimless detentions, send them to after-school clubs or additional classes, where there is an adult to direct them, and encourage them to engage with the activity.
- Collaborate as a staff. It is important that teachers work together to tackle disengaged learners. It is especially important in the secondary-school environment, where

students will have several different subject teachers and will frequently move from room to room (ample opportunity for wasting time and loitering in corridors). In this situation, students will feel they are more easily able to escape the issue of not completing work – they may not see the same teacher again for a week. Form tutors and heads of year can hopefully play a role in tightening the net around these individuals.

'Cling-ons'

Profile

Alice is 6. She is what you would describe as a 'needy' child. She is never far from your presence, and will follow you around the classroom anxiously until she gets your attention. She is quiet, and tends to veer away from interactions with other children – *you* are the focal point of her attention. She will often ask for you at break times, which has become a frustration for you. She is an emotional child: easily upset and frequently tearful. She still uses a comfort blanket. Her attainment is below average, though she works hard and is eager to please. Her verbal communication skills are quite limited, and you feel she may benefit from speech and language therapy. Alice's parents are committed to the school and take a big interest in her progress, although this is often overbearing.

Key concerns

- Student is showing signs of mild language and communication difficulties.
- Student is over-reliant on teacher attention.
- Student is not socializing with peers.
- Student is emotionally immature.
- Student's behaviour is putting undue pressure on the teacher.
- Overprotective nature of parents may be contributing to the problem.

The problem

At this young age, it is possible that Alice is going through a 'phase' – one that may hopefully right itself in the future; but it may also be a sign of delayed emotional and/or social development. The speech and language problems are of particular concern. Teachers are often the first to pick up on issues such as this, for they see the child in the context of other children – differences in maturity and development stand out clearly.

It can be difficult for teachers to cope with children such as Alice, for although she may not present a more obvious type of disruptive behaviour, her 'neediness' is placing considerable pressure on teacher time and attention – within a class of 30 or so other young children this can be very stressful. And of course, the teacher may want to be careful not reveal excessive frustration – knowing how easily upset Alice can be.

The issue of interfering, overprotective parents is a common one. In this case, it perhaps sheds some light on Alice's own anxieties. Conversations with parents/carers can often be very enlightening: their worries, concerns and attitudes may reflect their child's. Sometimes this can be to the detriment of the child's development. It is a frustrating scenario: the parents may be doing what they think is right/what they know; the teacher is having to deal with the in-class consequences. How do we do the best for such students without treading on each other's toes?

Strategies

- Refer to the SENCO. If you have concerns about a student's development, your key source of information, ideas and support will be the school SENCO. They will have the experience and knowledge required to identify possible SEN issues, and will be able to help you develop ways of managing the student's difficulties.
- Ensure work is accessible. Anxiety in the classroom can sometimes be a result of unexpressed difficulties with the level of work. Children will not always tell you if they are struggling – they will suffer in silence and become increasingly insecure. It is important to be vigilant, to make regular assessments, and be prepared to adapt tasks if necessary.

- Encourage small group socialization. For students that have difficulties interacting socially, create opportunities for them to take part in small group activities (of three to five individuals). For instance, have groups of students play boardgames during free time/tutorial periods. Interacting on a smaller scale is less daunting than the prospect of dealing with the whole class. You may be able to spend some time with a particular group, modelling good ways to interact.
- Organize a break-time buddy. Asking older/responsible students to take a vulnerable individual under their wing can be an effective way of enabling a child to feel more comfortable during breaks. Many schools operate some sort of 'buddy' system or peer mentoring scheme. If not, the Internet has a wealth of information about organizations that offer training and guidance.
- Set clear guidelines for gaining teacher attention. Reinforce positive ways of gaining attention (remaining in seat/putting hand up/etc.) with praise and encouragement. Redirect students to these approaches if they stray: 'I will come and look at your work, *when* you are sat in your seat.'
- Avoid losing patience. It is not always easy! Take a deep breath, count to ten, and remind yourself that the child is not deliberately trying to annoy you. At the same time, remember that you are not a machine – you are allowed to feel irritated by your students at times: learn to have control of how you express this to them.
- Negotiate with parents. Try to open up a dialogue between yourself and the child's parents/carers. Sharing strategy ideas and keeping each other informed of important issues and developments may be the key to a successful outcome. Do not go overboard. Do not, as one ex-colleague regretfully did, give out your home phone number!

Ringleaders

Profile

Javine is 13. She is always at the centre of something! An outgoing, bossy individual, she has developed a reputation among staff and students for being a 'troublemaker' – one that she is highly proud of. Her teachers are disappointed in her wayward tendencies. Her friends revere her. She leads a core group of friends, who are distinguishable by their matching hairstyles and mobile phones. They like boys, gossip and sticking two fingers up at authority – you suspect they also enjoy underage drinking in the park at night. They dislike learning (despite being bright students). Recently Javine has been coercing them into bunking lessons; and she has been temporarily excluded for that stalwart of disruptive behaviour, setting off the fire alarm. The rest of the year group are somewhat wary of Javine and her 'gang', for she has a tendency to react aggressively to anyone that she perceives is getting in her way/on her nerves. You are concerned that she is becoming increasingly disaffected, and is pulling her classmates down with her.

Key concerns

- Student uses disruptive behaviour to maintain an image.
- Student is influencing others into negative behaviour and attitude.
- Student has a disregard for the school environment and for education.
- Student is aggressive towards others, and exhibits threatening, bullying behaviour.
- Student is involved with anti-social behaviour and is becoming increasingly disaffected.
- Student is at risk: of exclusion, of further disaffection, of wasting her education and that of others.

The problem

This girl is on a downward spiral. Helping her, and the people she tries to drag down with her, is a difficult process. Social issues and friendship bonds can have a powerful hold over young people: a preoccupation, as has been mentioned several times in this book, with impressing friends, sticking by them, being part of a 'group'; and for some individuals, being top-dog. For those that fail, or struggle, or do not see the point of a school education, a social life is where they can prove themselves – and besides, its fun.

In this instance, Javine is a capable student that has lost interest in the formal purpose of school. She is smart enough to know what she is doing, but not mature enough to identify with the harmful long-term effects. Getting her to wake up to the negatives of her situation may be the key to changing her ways, but this could be a challenge in itself. 'Who is the real Javine?' is the painful question she will need to contemplate: what are the *real* issues behind her disaffection?

Dealing with the nucleus of the group may have an effect on the other students, but since there is no guarantee that Javine will mend her ways, the group will need to be addressed independently. It is not simply a matter of telling them to stay away from 'that nasty Javine' – that would only strengthen their bond. Besides, for every Javine that moves on there will be someone waiting to take her place. It is a matter of teaching, showing and encouraging these students to think independently and to take responsibility for themselves. They have long lived in the shadow and protection of their leader (sounds like a line from *Lord of the Rings*?); if they are to break free, they need something else to rely on ... self-esteem perhaps?

Strategies
- Clarify boundaries. Clear boundaries underpin effective behaviour management. Ensure that your students are clear about what is expected of them, and what will happen if they dissent. Students such as Javine are likely to push the boundaries regardless of how strongly you emphasize them, but by spelling them out you are being unambiguous and fair – she cannot argue with that (she will try, of course).
- Consistency across the school. If every teacher takes the same line on behaviour, then the challenge of crossing it becomes a lot more difficult. If specific individuals are

causing problems, it is important to share and consolidate strategies that are being used – either during a meeting or as a handout.

- Avoid confrontation. Rising to conflict, or reacting to poor behaviour in angry, power-seeking ways will do little to improve the situation. In fact, it will probably reinforce the idea that teachers are the enemy. Remain calm, be direct and firm and use phrases such as: 'I will talk to you when you are calm.' Focus on de-escalating the problem by sending the student on time-out, removing them from an audience, removing the cause of the problem, verbally calming them down or be willing to listen to their version of events.

- Emphasize choice. Giving students a choice about the outcome of their behaviour avoids backing them into corner and encourages them to take responsibility for their own actions: 'If you choose to continue kicking the table you will have to leave the room.'

- Use consequences that encourage students to reflect. Addressing challenging behaviour with a consequence is more effective if the consequence has an impact on the student. An individual such as Javine, who is at risk of losing her social conscience, may benefit from being made to contribute positively to the school or the community in some way – time spent in a care home, helping younger students or disadvantaged people. Activities such as these may improve her self-esteem, and give her something to think about.

- Anger management/self-esteem groups. I cannot over-emphasize the value of giving young people the knowledge and understanding to manage their own feelings and issues. Special groups, such as self-esteem or anger management, are on the increase in schools – hopefully this trend will continue. They are not a complete answer, they are part of a bigger process, but for some students they are extremely helpful.

- PSHCE. Likewise, PSHCE programmes afford many opportunities to explore issues relating to young people's feelings, attitudes and contributions to society. Increased access to this kind of discussion and information will enhance social awareness among the student population – and if ignorance is the road to disaster, awareness is surely the way to progress!

- Role models. Students like Javine will perhaps feel that the school system is against her, that teachers are an automatic enemy. But in every school, there is likely to be one fantastically strong, no-nonsense staff member: one that is able to straight-talk and empathize at the same time (in fact, if all teachers were like this, behaviour management would be easy!). An ally such as this – someone that has faith in the girl, but will not allow foul play – could make an enormous difference.

The easily led

Profile

Thomas is 8. He is a pleasant, friendly boy but recently has been getting into trouble on a regular basis. He has formed a friendship group with some of the more difficult students in the class, and you are concerned that he is being influenced by their wayward behaviour. You have caught him doing uncharacteristically silly things, like throwing stationery, or scribbling on his classmate's work – seemingly in a bid to impress them. When you tell him off, he is remorseful and upset. You have also noticed he has become more chatty during class work – his standard of work is beginning to slip. At break times he has got into trouble with the midday assistants for being cheeky – very unlike him. His parents are very concerned about the influence of his 'new friends', and have requested that he moves to another class.

Key concerns

- Student is being led into poor behaviour by others.
- Student is not making responsible choices about his actions.
- Student is not concentrating adequately on work.
- Student is at risk of underachieving.
- Student is preoccupied with impressing his peers.

The problem

Poor old Thomas! He only wants to belong ... the problem is, he is trying to belong to the 'wrong' crowd. It may be a temporary thing: friendships can be so transitory at that age. There is always the danger, however, that this is the start of the slippery slope – one taste of rebellion and he is hooked. It is important to intervene at an early stage, but this has to be done with care – a bombastic approach could push him further towards the dark side. Peer pressure is a powerful force.

It seems that he is flirting with trouble. So far his behaviours have been inappropriate but mild; but if he enjoys the reaction he gets from his mates, he may be tempted to go further. He is still innocent enough to be devastated by a telling-off – this suggests there is hope.

Thankfully his parents are on the case, but wanting to have him moved is not an ideal answer. The child has to learn to be his own person and to develop a sense of self-responsibility – he needs to learn to say 'no' and cope with whatever situation he is in. Otherwise he is prey for the next bad influence.

Strategies

- Avoid taking 'control'. Telling a student who they should and should not be friends with is likely to be counter-productive. Instead of making their choices for them, use tactics that encourage them to reflect on right and wrong – to make their own good decision. People tend to learn faster when they figure something out for themselves.
- Emphasize choice and praise good decisions. Use the language of choice when dealing with a problem, and give praise when the student makes an effort to ignore/avoid getting involved with inappropriate activity.
- Replace the thrill of gaining peer respect with positive experiences. If the student is looking for peer acceptance, promote ways in which they can do this positively – encourage them to be a role model for others.
- Get the student involved with activities that will raise their self-esteem: sports, drama, music, arts, etc.; it will provide them with an alternative means of feeling good about themselves.

- Discuss responsibility and peer pressure. Use PSHCE sessions to explore these issues. This will be of benefit to the whole class. You could even coordinate with other classes or year groups and organize a special assembly ... peer pressure awareness day?
- Rearrange seating plans. If groups of closely seated students are having a negative impact on one another, take control of the seating arrangements.
- Nurture alternative friendship groups. Arrange activities so that vulnerable, easily lead students are paired with individuals or groups that will exert a good influence.
- Set clear academic achievement goals. Be rigorous with your expectations of what the student is to do and by when; make it clear that you believe they are capable of doing the best, that they owe it to themselves, and that you will not give up on them, even if they try to give up on themselves.
- Mention the parents. The phrase 'Do I need to phone your parents and explain what you have done?' is often an effective bargaining stick. Avoid overuse, especially if you threaten it more then you do it – it will lose its potency.

Conclusion

So now all your classroom-management problems are solved, eh? Well ... maybe not, but hopefully what you have just read has given you the inspiration to shape up your practice and walk through that classroom door with renewed confidence. It may take some effort. Let's face it – reading a book is easy. The hard part is putting it into practice; but with patience and determination, effective classroom management can, and will, fall into place. The ideas I have provided in this book are by no means exhaustive, but hopefully provide some sound scaffolding from which you can develop your own personal way of doing the job.

The last point I wish to make is that, even when your students seem determined to destroy your efforts, they need you. They may not tell you this now, but somewhere down the line there will be a grown man saying, 'I remember Sir/Miss/Mrs. If it hadn't been for them ...' Teaching is about so much more than filling a young person's mind with the information necessary to get them through exams. From you, they can learn about themselves: how to give and receive respect, how to manage feelings and responses to the world around them, how to get the most out of the opportunities that come their way. And for some of your most vulnerable students, you may be the one person in their life that can give them a consistent, stable and positive environment. It is a daunting responsibility, but one that can be rich with reward.